LESSONS
FROM A
BEDSIDE

Breda Casserly is a healthcare chaplain in the Galway Hospice Foundation, in Renmore, Galway, a position she fulfilled full time for eleven years before moving to a support role in spring 2021. She is a graduate of NUI Galway and All Hallows College, Dublin, with postgraduate degrees in Pastoral Theology and Cross-Professional Supervision. She teaches on spiritual/soul pain for the Postgraduate Diploma in Nursing (Palliative Care) at NUI Galway.

Lessons from a Bedside is her first book.

LESSONS

FROM A

BEDSIDE

WISDOM FOR LIVING

BREDA CASSERLY

HACHETTE
BOOKS
IRELAND

First published in Ireland in 2021 by
HACHETTE BOOKS IRELAND

1

Cataloguing in Publication Data is available from the British Library

ISBN 9781529341973

Typeset in Sabon by redrattledesign.com

Printed and bound in Great Britain by
Clays, Elcograf S.p.A

Hachette Books Ireland policy is to use papers that are natural, renewable
and recyclable products and made from wood grown in sustainable forests.
The logging and manufacturing processes are expected to conform to the
environmental regulations of the country of origin.

Hachette Books Ireland
8 Castlecourt Centre
Castleknock
Dublin 15, Ireland

A division of Hachette UK Ltd
Carmelite House, 50 Victoria Embankment, EC4Y 0DZ

www.hachettebooksireland.ie

This book is dedicated to the memory of
Cliona Keavney, a beloved friend and former
physiotherapist at Galway Hospice. Thinking of
her children and her parents.

To remember is a noble and good thing.

AUTHOR NOTE

As we go to print on this book, we have been living through the Coronavirus pandemic for one year. We are experiencing a time of active history, possibly the most uncertain and unsettling of our lives. A time when we are acutely aware that we are dependent rather than independent people.

Over the past year the sands of our lives have shifted under our feet and have exposed how fragile and vulnerable our human lives really are. Being constantly advised to 'stay at home', 'stay safe' and 'physically distance' has impacted our emotional wellbeing. It is on the inside where the most significant battles are waged. Daily temperature taking, protective clothing, and physical distancing from patients, families and colleagues has left little space for healthy human interaction which has been a challenge for us all in the hospice. In my role as chaplain, this new and necessary way of living which was thrust upon us feels so alien to my soul.

One particular day stands out: a young man was admitted to the hospice from his home at around eleven o'clock one morning for end-of-life care. Doctor Camilla asked me to visit him, saying his time was very short. Before entering his hospice room, I needed to put on my gown, gloves, mask, and goggles. Can you just imagine how I looked to this vulnerable, fragile young man, who had just come from his home, grappling with the news that he was coming towards the end of his life? My first instinct was to apologise to him for sitting at a distance and for wearing protective clothing that did not allow even a glimpse of the person behind it. I wanted to reassure him that I was Breda, the chaplain.

Our facial expressions can and do reveal the

the empathy we have for others, and most people need the reassurance of a kind face or the touch of a hand when they are sick and vulnerable. Being denied this basic but hugely important human need has been one of the tougher elements of this pandemic. However, kindness and love has emerged among people that sustains and carries us through this time. Conversations have a depth and an empathy that reveals the human behind the mask. We need and find comfort in the shelter of each other.

Breda Casserly, March 2021

CONTENTS

FOREWORD

For many, 'hospice' is a scary word and they believe it means the end, but this is not the case. Hospice care (or palliative care) has changed significantly over the past thirty years. It is about living well and comfortably right to the end. You will always find a warm welcome and a smile from the team of staff and volunteers at Galway Hospice. They know the challenges that those facing a life-limiting illness have to deal with and are always there to provide support and to brighten their days.

The founder of the modern hospice movement was Dame Cicely Saunders. After the Second World War, she began volunteering at a hospice in London and while there, she became increasingly frustrated with what she felt was doctors' ambivalence towards terminally ill patients – those who couldn't be cured – and concluded that her best chance for showing a better way would be to become a physician herself. In 1951, at the age of thirty-three, she became a medical student. When she obtained her medical degree in 1957, she became the first modern doctor to devote her career to dying patients. Her work was influenced by the experiences and wisdom of early hospices in medieval Europe when the care for the sick and the dying was deeply holistic, focusing on the spiritual aspect of pain and suffering. Those living in the middle ages realised that pain is primarily a physical and emotional experience centred in our physical body. They believed that it was possible to have a more peaceful death if the spiritual pain of a dying person was dealt with directly and with compassionate support. They understood that having a realistic acceptance of death throughout life allowed for a more joyous life and a more peaceful death. Dame Cicely confirmed her support for a similar approach when she said, 'Our work is to alter the character of this inevitable process so that it is not seen as a defeat of living but as a possible achievement in dying, an intensely individual achievement for the patient.' Sadly in today's world, we often deny the existence of death until we are facing it. We have a tendency to ignore, repress and self-medicate the spiritual pain accumulated during life. This can mean that when serious illness occurs it can become a time of suffering known as 'total' or 'spiritual pain'.

I came to understand the hospice concept a number of years before beginning my work there when a family member was diagnosed with a life-limiting illness and struggled to cope with the diagnosis. As a family, we tried to provide care and support at home but we were not equipped to provide the clinical and emotional support that was needed. Our general practitioner suggested an admission to our local hospice for symptom control and, as we were exhausted and struggling to provide the care that was needed both physically and emotionally, we welcomed the idea. This is where I was first exposed to the holistic nature of hospice care. The team at the hospice created a supportive environment where fears and concerns could be aired and discussed and, in my opinion, worked miracles. They got the physical symptoms under control, but more importantly provided the emotional support that eased the mental stress and assisted with coming to terms with the prognosis. This resulted in discharge after a six-week stay and enabled my family member to live well within the limitations of their illness for a further six months afterwards. This positive experience changed my perception of hospice care and opened my eyes to what I now understand about the care provided by the hospice teams.

Hospice care is not about giving up, it is about living the best quality of life possible while living with a life-limiting illness, and my experience of the care provided by our local hospice definitely confirms this concept. At Galway Hospice we help people to live each of life's moments to the fullest, with the ones who matter most. We are about hope, caring and going the extra mile to make life the best it can be. Our staff and volunteers work tirelessly to bring comfort and solace to the patients and their families at what is probably the most difficult and frightening time in their lives. They truly demonstrate the palliative care experience: to cure occasionally, to relieve often, to comfort always.

Hospice is about providing a safe space for both the individual living with the life-limiting illness and their family and loved ones. At Galway Hospice our motto is 'every moment matters' and the team at the hospice work to ensure that our patients and families get to spend quality time with each other to make sure that every moment does matter. This includes providing the best quality medical and clinical care possible to ensure that patients' physical symptoms are effectively managed and also providing emotional and psychological support to our patients and their families at a difficult and frightening time.

Dame Cicely Saunders describes the modern hospice as 'a resting place for travellers but above all it is concerned with journeys of discovery. For patients a discovery of what is most lasting and important for them as they unravel some knots of deceit and regret.' Over the past number of years since coming to work at the hospice, I have seen many patients and their families experience this journey of discovery as they coped with their prognoses. For some it has involved sharing their story to help support the work of the hospice and to help others and for others it has been about dealing with issues that have been causing them emotional distress all their lives. Others will strive to achieve goals that they set for themselves – it may be about having a target of being there for a final family celebration or to be there for the birth of a grandchild or to celebrate other significant milestones, such as an anniversary.

The people I meet and the stories they share inspire me on a daily basis; they allow us into their lives at a very challenging time and on occasion share their innermost thoughts and fears with the team at the hospice. Frequently we can do something practical to assist and help them but often, it is about providing a safe, supportive environment where they can give voice to their innermost thoughts and fears. Sometimes it is just about being there to hold their hand, supporting them on their journey.

The team at the hospice spend time getting to know those who are being treated as individuals as well as patients. This is essential in enabling us to provide the support they need so that they can achieve the best outcome possible while living with a terminal illness. I can recall one such patient that I met when they were referred to our Inpatient Unit for end-of-life care. The patient had been bedbound prior to admission to the hospice and even required assistance with positioning while in bed. Over the course of a number of weeks, the team at the hospice worked with the patient to assist with managing their symptoms and putting a plan in place to assist with mobility, as this patient had a goal of being at home to support her daughter when she had her first child. This woman had had a challenging life even before being diagnosed with her illness, but she did not let it defeat her; she was determined to be there to support her daughter when she needed her, and with the support of the hospice team she achieved her goal. Unfortunately, her time with her grandchild was limited but it was quality time and it meant a lot to both her and her immediate family. We received a lovely thank-you card from them after she passed and I will always recall one comment in that card, 'Thank you for enabling her to exceed her expectations.'

The work of the hospice does not end when someone dies; we continue to be there to provide support to family and friends while they deal with the loss of a loved one if they need it. This knowledge can also provide support to the patient as they progress on their journey, as they know that there will be a support system there to assist their family while they grieve.

Very few of us go through life without facing difficulties and many of us choose to push these to one side while coping with a busy day-to-day life trying to make ends meet. It is only when faced with a time limit on our life that we may be forced to deal with these unresolved issues so that we can let go and find emotional peace. Dame Cicely describes this in her writings when she states, 'Many of us have sensed that an inner journey has taken place and that a person nearing the end of life has found peace.' This peace may be simply reassuring a homeless man that he is in a safe place where he will be cared for to the end, or it may involve lengthy conversations with patients and families as they work through their concerns and issues and seek to find a resolution before time runs out. You will find evidence of this in the stories told throughout this book. Time and again, we see examples of mental pain being soothed when physical symptoms are alleviated. A temporary release from pain can also make it easier for the team to make a connection with the patient.

Simply listening itself can also have a therapeutic impact on the patient; it can give them the chance to talk, which can form an important part of the healing process. I know that the stories and lessons that you will read about in the following chapters are life-affirming and demonstrate the importance of living well to the end. I would like to commend Breda on taking the time to document these important stories and I hope that they will inspire you as they have inspired us here at the hospice.

Don't count the days, make the days count.

Mary Nash, CEO Galway Hospice Foundation, January 2021

INTRODUCTION

T'wenty-five years ago I had a deep experience of God, which gifted me with a great desire to serve Him and my fellow human beings. It's a private experience I've treasured in my heart and leaned on throughout my life, an experience that really changed me and my view of the world.

At that time I was in the handmade chocolate business, as the owner of Leonidas Chocolates in Galway. I felt safe and comfortable within my business knowledge and the company's success. But at the same time I felt unsettled within myself, feeling that there must be more to life than what I was experiencing, more challenge for personal growth.

I now understand my inner turmoil was a desire for a deeper satisfaction in life. This is often called 'hope pain', an emotional pain that one experiences when there is a lack of hope and where one asks, 'What does the future hold for me?' I was also experiencing something curious that I know now to be 'meaning pain', where it's natural to ask oneself, 'Why am I here?'

I responded to these questions and many others by studying Theology as an undergraduate at NUI Galway, for two years, then three years undertaking postgraduate studies in Pastoral Theology at All Hallows College, Dublin, giving myself time to explore my life in a more meaningful and deeper way. I didn't necessarily feel called to a religious life or order, however, I did feel the need to be part of a praying community so I joined the Secular Franciscan Order as a lay Franciscan.

I remember it as an especially challenging time, because I continued to work in the business, albeit with the support of a very good team. Despite these challenges, it gave very good balance to my life at the time. I had studied Theology specifically to explore my own understanding of God and to nourish myself spiritually. I had no great future plans to work in this field but was leaving myself open to if and where God might call me.

There is a very beautiful old saying, 'When the student is ready, the master arrives', and in a sense this is what happened for me. Having completed my studies and returned to work in the chocolate business full time, a simple telephone call came, on a very dark, wet and windy autumn evening. It was a local diocesan priest, Father Noel, who I knew very well from my community.

'Breda, I had a thirty-five-year-old mother of two young children come and visit me a couple of days ago,' he explained. 'Orla is a patient in your local hospital in Galway; she has been given a cancer diagnosis and was told she has just a few months to live. As a child she had received the Sacrament of Baptism, but never received the further sacraments of First Confession, First Holy Communion and Confirmation, and has asked to receive them before her death. What I'm asking of you is can you visit with her to prepare her to receive the sacraments?'

I was taken aback. At the time, the thought of

visiting a hospital made me very uncomfortable. And I'd never prepared someone for the sacraments before, let alone for the end of life. I was struck by the huge contrast between our lives – mine was so full of possibilities, preparing for a busy festive season of selling lots of chocolate gifts, while hers was sadly ebbing away. I had no idea how to do what was being asked of me, or what my approach would be, or what I could ever offer her.

'You know, I'm just so busy preparing for Christmas in the business,' I told Father Noel. 'I have little free time.'

But Father Noel wouldn't accept any excuses. 'Stop all this nonsense and just go,' he said simply. 'This young woman needs your help.'

I am eternally grateful to this priest who had the grace and vision to push me out of my comfort zone. He was probably unaware that he was in great measure helping me face my own deep spiritual and emotional pain.

What I had not shared with Father Noel was that my sister Teresa had died in the very same hospital where Orla was now a patient. Teresa's husband, Paddy Joe, had also died there, some years later. My sister, also a young mother, had been given a similar cancer diagnosis to Orla, and passed away at Christmas time.

Fifteen years before Teresa, my sister Mamie had died at the age of twenty-six when her daughter was just two weeks old. Mamie had been diagnosed with a cancerous brain tumour in the early stages of her pregnancy.

My conversation with Father Noel about Orla brought memories of my sisters and the last days of their lives rushing back to me. And I had been with both Teresa and Paddy Joe at the moments of their deaths, an experience I was not in a hurry to revisit.

Indeed I had a deep fear of death and an even stronger fear of a cancer diagnosis. I was just fourteen years old when Mamie died and at that young age had the stark and uncomfortable realisation that a young person can die. It really brought me face to face with my own mortality, which I believe is a very common reaction.

Needless to say I had a sleepless night after that phone call, having agreed with Father Noel to think about his request to visit Orla. I tossed and turned, listening to the wind and rain through the dark of night, while I searched my mind for any excuse not to visit the hospital. I was consumed with fear for two days and made a decision to telephone the hospital chaplain. The chaplain is there for everyone, whether they have faith or not. It doesn't matter if you've never been to church, or never intend to go. Some people turn to the chaplain because they are religious or they want to explore their spirituality. Others, for whom religion is not important, look to the chaplain to be an accepting and positive companion as they travel what might become a tough journey through their illness. So I phoned Father Tommy, who I knew as a hospital-ordained chaplain and indeed as a customer who came to our shop regularly to purchase chocolates, to seek his advice.

'I've been asked to visit Orla – is there any necessity for me to come in? Would you prefer to work with her?' I asked, hoping he would answer in the affirmative.

But I didn't get the answer I wanted. 'I'd really welcome your support to work with this young woman,' he replied. 'Maybe you could visit her as soon as possible, while she still has some quality of life.'

A day later, I phoned the clinical nurse manager on Orla's ward, who responded positively.

'Orla is really looking forward to meeting you, will you be in today?' she asked.

Hesitantly, I made a decision to face my fear. I hoped that, as well as offering some help to Orla, I would also find some healing and peace through this experience.

Now I know that life will present many opportunities for healing at the right moment and through the right situations. And though this process is often painful, the reward is great. We need to be alert to those moments and hear them with our spiritual ears, and receive them with our spiritual hearts. Though reluctant to hear the healing opportunity in Father Noel's request, life somehow presented all the opportunities in a gentle way to support my own spiritual healing. I had been offered an emotionally painful but grace-filled opportunity to face my spiritual pain: one that ended up really opening my heart to a ministry in a hospice.

The next four weeks were to change my life forever. Although managing my work commitments during such a busy time stretched me both mentally and physically at times, the experience with Orla expanded my soul to a deep understanding of spiritual and emotional pain.

Both Orla and I became teachers for each other, as she shared her life story and her deep soul pain around letting go of her family, in particular her two young children. When we talk to patients at end of life about 'letting go' of people, we are trying to help them process the idea of leaving these people behind, allowing them to share their concerns and worries, and reassuring them that things will be okay for them after they're gone. And often, patients are simply looking for permission just to let go of life to death.

'I was awake early this morning, Breda, thinking of my children,' Orla noted one morning I was with her. 'How do I let go of them? My heart is broken. I can't understand how God would let me die. Will they remember me? Will they even remember they had a mum? No one could care for them as much as I could.'

Any words of mine in response would be inadequate and could not offer any consolation. Those were big questions, which no human could answer. But Orla was expressing a need to be heard at a deep level, and listening to her empathetically and actively was the best thing I could do for her. I realised through this process that there is a window of work at the end of life that is so important to the soul for healing before death. This soul work presents a reality to the patient, and indeed their family, that to face death means to face the ending of hopes and plans, and an understanding that sadness around that reality is appropriate and should be faced and shared. A patient can and does experience their own unique grief at letting go to face their death. This work calls for a listener, and can give a greater freedom and strength to the patient in facing what is to come.

'What is the purpose in life? I grew up, became a mother, and now, I'm going to die,' she said, almost disbelievingly. My sense was that Orla was trying to search at a very deep level within herself.

Through many conversations, we explored together the meaning and purpose in life, and truth be told, we realised it was difficult to come to any reasonable conclusion. It's difficult to understand why a young woman would die at the age of thirty-five, leaving two young children behind.

We came to understand that life and death are not opposite, that mind and body are not separate, and that emotional pain is felt in all areas of the body. We talked about how Orla's physical pain was affecting her emotionally, but also how the opposite was true – her emotional pain was affecting her physical pain.

On Christmas week, in an isolated room, with the support of the hospital chaplain, Father Tommy, Orla received her much-longed-for sacraments. The moment was joyful on the surface, but beneath was a profound sadness with a lingering awareness of limited time. Later that evening, Orla, her family and myself reflected on our journey together as we brought closure to what now had become our soul friendship; it was emotionally painful but filled with gratitude that her spiritual need was fulfilled.

I recall Orla was wearing a beautiful white dress, a gift from her mother. She reached out her hand to me.

'Will you stay with me, Breda?' she asked softly. 'Will you teach me how to pray?'

I felt very inadequate in the face of this request, as it was difficult enough for me to pray in my own life. But I realised that Orla's desire to pray demonstrated that she needed a sense of comfort for her final weeks.

As I walked back towards the city after leaving

the hospital, with Christmas lights shining and music filling the cold winter air, I had a deep sense that the ache of the heart is indeed very lonely, and the inner worlds of all of us need hospitality. Even though I hadn't felt confident in my ability to help Orla when I first visited her, I had offered her the opportunity to share her deepest pain and fear about what she faced.

Orla passed away some weeks later. I attended her funeral, quietly seated at the back of the church. As I drove the two-hour journey home afterwards I reflected on the incredible journey life had presented to me and felt a deep gratitude for the grace and strength to stay the course with Orla. She had become and continues to be the most important teacher in my life.

Over that Christmas period, I addressed in good measure my grief at the loss of my lovely sisters. I allowed myself to reflect on my memories with both – Teresa's passion for country music and the many hours of her teaching me to drive, and Mamie who, as a nurse, had such a kind sense of care for others.

I thought of their love for their very young children, and what unbearable sadness they must have felt in their final days at the thought of leaving them.

For the first time, I gave myself permission to really feel the pain at these losses. I talked with members of my family about their lives and the sadness we all felt. This unburdening and sharing with my family made me more settled in myself than I had been in years.

Although I only knew her for a short time, my friendship with Orla has impacted greatly on my life. I had grown emotionally and spiritually through those brief months and felt an inner calling to ministry as a result. I began to explore the idea of becoming a pastoral care chaplain as a lay person.

A fortnight after Orla's death, I bumped into a local priest, Father Hugh, on Shop Street in Galway.

'How was Christmas for you, Breda?' he said.

'From a business perspective it was great, but I found for myself, there was a lot of unrest within me,' I admitted candidly.

I shared with him my work with Orla, and my realisation that I'd like to explore the role of healthcare chaplain further. My mind was whirling with questions about where my future lay. Should

I leave my business, after twenty years of success? Should I embark on an unknown future?

But Father Hugh was very encouraging of the idea of me exploring this new path. 'I myself have studied Clinical Pastoral Education at Kerry General Hospital. The director of the programme, Father John, has written his doctoral thesis on spiritual pain. Truly, it's an excellent programme. And Tralee is such a lovely town.'

I still recall vividly my first trip to Tralee to meet with Father John, leaving home at 6 a.m. with a strong sense that this journey would change the direction of my life forever. I was also apprehensive – my life was currently comfortable and secure, so it was nerve-wracking to consider making a change to something more unknown. I remember stopping in Castleisland at a bakery serving early breakfast, and having a chat with the waitress, telling her I was presenting for interview, and hearing her kind words of encouragement and affirmation. Leaving the café, I thought, a cup of coffee is only a cup of coffee, but when served with kindness, it is indeed a lovely experience.

Father John was welcoming and encouraging and offered great support through the next ten months as I began the process of selling the business, letting go of twenty years of working in a busy but very happy career. I signed the legal document to hand over my business to its new owners on 5 December 2007, and drove to Tralee on 31 December 2007 to begin studies in Clinical Pastoral Education. I had a whole new energy, thinking about what the future held for me.

I knew that serving God and people would not be easy, but had no real idea about what I had let myself in for. In particular I did not realise it would mean the mixture of joy and suffering involved in travelling to the depths of who I am as a human being.

I believe the distance we travel in our own lives is the only distance we can travel with another, and this in essence is the core teaching of Clinical Pastoral Education to prepare students for healthcare chaplaincy, which is centred on offering pastoral care as a safe, confidential and professional process that helps people to explore, reflect and resolve fears and difficulties in their spiritual and emotional life. It was in this safe and contained environment, under the supervision of professionals in pastoral education, that we were encouraged through group therapy to explore old and hidden emotional wounds, bringing emotional pain to the level where it could be shared, heard and healed. If we looked at and addressed our own spiritual and emotional pain first, we would be able to make ourselves emotionally available to patients and families. It was through this process that I addressed my fear of death and illness.

This deep, reflective work at soul level is very emotionally painful, but when these emotions are heard with empathy and compassion, a space opens up in our souls for great healing. Soul reflection is a way of transformation – if we are becoming more whole, then the people we are listening to in our chaplaincy work are becoming a bit more whole too, and it only stands to reason that our society, in a small but significant way, is also becoming more whole. I truly believe that there is a flame in each of us that warms the other. This soul work is a process and continues through spiritual direction or clinical supervision as we continue to work in ministry.

Many people embark on this journey of deep soul reflection when they reach the end of their lives. When we come to face our own dying, most of us will want to know that we are loved and valued. We may experience a sense of disconnection from our previous life, when we lived in an active and healthy way. This can be very scary, and patients say it so often. We may feel disconnected from our physical body, which has gone through many changes through illness and the treatments given to try to cure it. We might find our lives have become very limited in our interaction with people outside of family due to less physical energy and activity. All of this can cause a crisis of identity, sometimes not recognising the person we have become. Yet, in the midst of all of this, there is a longing to connect meaningfully with others, to share the story of a life that was lived to the full before serious illness had in some way changed our identity and became the only conversation we seem to have with others. And it is the role of a healthcare chaplain to help people on this journey.

I have now worked through eleven years of pastoral care ministry at Galway Hospice, an eighteen-bed facility situated in the suburban area of Renmore, Galway, with the salty sea air of the nearby Atlantic ocean blowing through its garden. There, I am privileged to support people as they address the big questions of meaning, identity, connection and belief, which is indeed the process of soul reflection and spiritual care.

Boundaries are very important in caring work, and a part of good professional working. It's a learning process to be totally involved and totally detached at exactly the same moment, but it's a necessary skill in chaplaincy. Nonetheless it is inevitable that I will be affected by my work – I believe I would not be doing my work properly if I wasn't. I can and do feel sadness because of my closeness to people who experience sadness. But I feel joy and hope too. And through my work I have become very aware that our most significant insights can happen when we face the end of our life.

Through the pages of this book I would like to share with you my work of accompanying patients and their families at the end of their life, and the many invaluable lessons I have learned through this privileged ministry at Galway Hospice: lessons covering spiritual pain, forgiveness, loss and grief, the importance of story and making memories.

In some measure, these lessons will provide healing for us and in turn help us to live life in a more meaningful and reflective way, resulting in a life well lived for ourselves, with others, and indeed wider society. It is useful to ask yourself, is the life you are living now the same as the life that wants to live within you?

When telling stories of my patients, I have often changed names and significant details. However, there are a couple of exceptions to this. Caroline Egan and her sister Marie kindly gave me permission to write about the meeting I describe with her. Harry and Moya, Paula O'Donnell's husband and daughter, have kindly allowed me to share her story. Ann Moran and her son Dermot share the story of their beloved husband and father, John.

I will quote some Christian texts, and if you are not from the Christian tradition, I encourage you to find corresponding passages in other sacred writings or in secular literature.

This book presents a small handful of the myriad experiences and stories that I have encountered through my work, viewed through the lenses of different themes, starting with spiritual pain. I would like to express my warmest appreciation of all of the patients, families, staff and volunteers at Galway Hospice, for this book, which I hope will demystify people's perceptions of hospices, has grown out of my relationship with this very special place.

CHAPTER 1

Spiritual Pain

What is pain? This is a difficult question to answer: the experience of pain is complex and involves many different levels. Much has been written on ways to alleviate pain in the body as a result of illness and disease. And in recent times there has been great interest in the care of the whole person – on mind, body, spirit and emotion, rather than just the illness or disease of the body. Spiritual pain is a component of the psycho-social factors that contribute to a person's experience of pain and as a result should be identified and treated in the same way that physical pain is.

Physical pain can be exacerbated by non-physical causes which can include fear, anxiety, feelings of guilt, grief, loss of control and unmet spiritual needs, to name but a few. An English doctor called Dame Cicely Saunders, founder of the modern hospice movement, coined the term 'total pain' to describe pain that is all-encompassing of mind, body, emotion and spirit in a person facing the end of their life, a pain that is also experienced by the person's loved ones. It is important to recognise that spiritual issues can and do impact on how a person deals with physical pain.

Spirituality is a term that means different things to different people. Religion and faith might be part of someone's spirituality, but spirituality isn't always religious. A classic definition of spirituality is the search for meaning and direction in life. Beyond the physical, it is a beckoning towards something greater than the self, and is both within and beyond the person. Some may refer to it as God, Allah, Buddha or another religious figure. Some may regard spirituality as the wonder of nature. Whatever way it is interpreted, it is a resource for strength, guidance and support on life's journey.

Most people will experience forms of physical and emotional pain at some stage in their lives. However, spiritual pain also affects all of us, especially at times of challenge and transition through different stages of life. I am fortunate to work in a hospice environment where spiritual pain is considered of equal importance to physical and emotional pain and documented on each patient's admission chart. This means we treat each patient in a holistic way – addressing the body, mind and spirit. Spiritual pain is the pain that comes from the hidden areas of our lives. Frequently when experiencing physical pain, a person is asked to score their pain from one to ten to indicate the severity of pain and give a medical professional an idea of how to respond to it. Although there is no such score for spiritual pain, it is still very real and can impact our physical and emotional health. Thus, managing spiritual pain may help to reduce physical pain or other symptoms.

A diagnosis of total pain would treat the person from a physical, emotional, social, and spiritual perspective. In 500 BC, Greek physician Hippocrates, the father of medicine, asked, 'How is it that pain and suffering heals?' He recognised that alleviation of pain is good – but not the ultimate good. From time to time a person experiences transformation out of tragedy.

People may experience spiritual pain as feelings of hopelessness or fear, regret or guilt. As Richard Groves, author and co-founder of the Sacred Art of Living Center in Oregon, states, it is often broken down into four categories:

1. Meaning – the person may begin to feel there is no longer any meaning in their life, their relationships or the world around them.

2. Forgiveness – the person may struggle with the idea of forgiving others, God or themselves.

3. Relatedness – the person may have difficulty dealing with relationships, whether good or bad.

4. Hopelessness – the person may experience a feeling of hopelessness in their life, feeling everything is pointless in their existence.

Nowadays, spiritual pain can often be referred to as emotional pain or indeed soul pain. I have found reference to spiritual pain dating back to thirteenth-century Ireland, and have no doubt there are earlier references. In *The Celtic Book of Living and Dying*, a book about ancient Celtic wisdom, there is a reference to Irish hermit and monk Abbott Fintan, and a quotation, 'May you have the commitment to know what has hurt you, to allow it to come closer to you, and in the end, become one with you.' We all have our hidden wounds and at some stage in our lives we will acknowledge and bring our wound to the surface and shine a light on it, lean into the pain and be healed through that same wound. A time comes when our subconscious will say, 'Now it is my turn', and will find a way to express its repressed emotions and feelings.

People usually experience spiritual pain when faced with a particular life crisis that challenges their core values and beliefs about how things are supposed to be and causes them to lose a sense of meaning or purpose in life. Working through our mind's basement of painful wounds, though not easy, can be most beneficial for our mental health. As the saying goes, 'The best way around is through'. Processing spiritual pain allows the person to experience a new peace, a richness and a depth in their living and dying.

Spiritual pain can sometimes signal the need for a new or different direction in life, and the possibility of personal growth. It is important to listen to all of this pain, to process what is going on in your life and allow life to open up a new path of growth and transformation.

One Saturday afternoon, I was supporting a family to help them celebrate a fiftieth wedding anniversary. In hospice we are always very open to celebrating the special occasions and milestones of our patients' lives; they bring family together and, in this environment, special care is taken of both the patient and family.

Brendan was a patient with us at hospice. He had worked in forestry and regaled us with memories from his working life. He had great stories in particular around Hurricane Debbie, and the sheer devastation of the woodland areas that he bore witness to.

Brendan was now entering the terminal phase of his illness, and had expressed a need to celebrate this milestone wedding anniversary with his wife and family. It was an afternoon filled with stories and memories, tears and laughter, prayer, music and food – meaningful things done meaningfully. The family looked over old photos, noting the contrast between the original wedding photographs, taken in black and white, and through the years how the colour drifted into the photos as their family grew. They took many photos that day too. There was a sense of fulfilment as I made my way to say my usual evening goodbyes to the nursing staff.

But as I pulled my coat on to leave, Mary, the clinical nurse manager, put her head around the door.

'Have you time to visit Hugh in Room 4 before you go?' she asked. 'He is very tearful and his mood appears low.'

Hugh's Story

I'd first met Hugh the previous week, when he was admitted to hospice for end-of-life care. A reserved, gentle man in his early fifties, Hugh came from a midland county, and had moved west over twenty years ago. As I sat quietly on a chair beside his bed, Hugh looked at me intently with eyes filled with tears.

'I know my days are numbered, but there is something I need to talk about,' he began. 'It's heavy in my heart these days.'

Hugh shared a story from when he was nineteen years of age.

'One evening my girlfriend told me that she was pregnant with my baby,' he recalled. 'I felt quite nervous bringing this news to my mother. However, I was not at all prepared for her reaction.'

He was asked to leave the family home that night and have no future contact with his parents, siblings, or indeed the extended family. He moved to the west coast of Ireland, where he married his girlfriend, and his daughter was born. He attempted to make family contact over the next couple of years, with no success.

'I found it hard to deal with this family rejection, and all the emotions involved in that,' Hugh reflected. 'All I could do was to not think about what had happened and try to get on with my life.' He acknowledged that he had blocked out his many painful emotions.

'I threw myself into my career, and to be honest,

there were times when I just drank to forget about the past,' he admitted. He felt that, on reflection, his experience of disconnection from his family of origin at a relatively young age had affected all relationships thereafter, in particular with his three daughters, who were by then grown up.

'One day out of the blue, I had a telephone call from a cousin,' he said. 'She told me that my mother had passed away two months earlier. That was so painful, and as we never talked of my mother in our family, I found it sort of difficult to share this news with my wife.'

Hugh poured out his deep soul pain, at times expressing compassion for his mother.

Sitting up in his bed, hands in his lap, he reflected, 'I suppose it was the time that was in it. Things were certainly tough for us, but I'm sure it was hard for my mother as well. She was living through those times, where there was a huge worry about what other people in the village thought, and shame on the family was a very genuine concern.'

In a spirit of deep compassion, he had already forgiven her. He wondered if he might meet with her after death. Even now, he still had a longing to be mothered by her.

The simple giving of a listening presence allowed Hugh time and space to express his long-held pain and allowed the soul itself to act. I believe for sure that in the depth of each person there is a knowing that desires our deepest healing. As the low evening summer sun shone through into Hugh's room, the exhaustion of expressing his emotions was visible as he closed his eyes to rest. The call of his soul was answered and he died quietly twenty-four hours later.

Not everything in Hugh's life was resolved, and not all of his spiritual pain was healed. It rarely is for any of us. We give little time in our lives to process emotional pain, and it always feels preferable to put things at the back of our minds. But this pain will always try and find a way to express itself, and sooner or later, it will surface. This had been the case for Hugh, and he had processed it as best he could by expressing this pain through telling me his story.

We are all worthy of a safe place and space to deal with unresolved issues and speak about important relationships without being judged.

Everyone is on a spiritual journey from the

moment they are born and from that journey, we feel pain and, in turn, we grow. Our society doesn't often emphasise this journey, so we have a difficult time dealing with the pain when it becomes too much to handle. When you acknowledge and accept your pain as simple growth and begin to process your life experiences, you release any struggle and give permission for the journey ahead. After all, we are all just trying to find a sense of home inside ourselves; to feel what it is to be a human being, to feel safe in our own bodies and to be part of a community.

For people living with a serious or life-limiting illness, finding ways to cope with one's illness and feelings, with the help of others if necessary, can make a big difference to one's sense of control and purpose. It benefits us to reconnect with those very simple and ordinary aspects of life that have, in the past, brought us a sense of depth or significance. These reconnections vary greatly from person to person, but rekindling old friendships, sitting and enjoying a cup of tea and reminiscing about the past, or enjoying a family get-together are savoured anew, and can bring about a richness in a way that it didn't before.

Through his hospice stay, Hugh eventually

became aware of having emotional needs alongside his medical needs – he felt the need to speak about his wounds from the past. He got a true sense that how he felt emotionally was every bit as important as how he felt physically.

Stephen's Story

I met with Stephen on his admission day to hospice, as his wife, Mary, unpacked his personal belongings from a simple suitcase. Chief among Stephen's concerns in that moment was getting on top of his physical pain.

Through the following days, Stephen, having settled well into his comfortable room and now receiving his much-needed pain medication, slowly began to share his life story in a shy and quiet way. He was tall and broad-shouldered, with the physicality of a man who had worked hard for most of his life, even amid his illness. With a lovely lilt, he began to talk.

'I'm very fortunate,' he observed. 'I have a lovely wife who takes good care of me, and I have two wonderful daughters, two fantastic sons, and five grandchildren. Let me show you their photos.'

He took photographs from his wallet to show me his family with great pride.

'They're coming to visit this weekend,' he revealed. 'I can't wait to see the grandkids. They're great for keeping a person young at heart.'

It was springtime and as Stephen observed nature through the window, one morning he quietly asked if it was possible to go into the garden, as he longed for a breath of fresh air. Wrapping up warm, we made our way through the conservatory into the garden for a gentle walk. He stared into the distance with his brow furrowed.

'They're nice daffodils, Breda,' he said, almost so quietly that it felt like he was talking to himself. He savoured the moment, inhaling lungfuls of the fresh air.

As we returned through the conservatory, Stephen turned to me suddenly.

'Would it be okay if we sat for a moment, just to enjoy the garden?' he said. In that moment, I sensed his need to talk.

'I'm thinking of a friend today,' he admitted. 'I miss him, and wish he were here.' He began to share the story of his childhood friend Matt. They grew up together on small hillside farms, beginning school on the same day and enjoying local sport together through the years.

'One summer's day, we were on the bog,' he

recalled. 'We made a decision, the two of us, that come the autumn, when all the farm work was done, we would go to England and make a good life for ourselves. Through that summer we saved every penny, looking forward to a new life. We made a promise to look out for each other no matter what the circumstances. We would help each other in good times and bad times.'

On arrival in England, both Matt and Stephen found construction work in London. They enjoyed the showband dances in the Galtymore ballroom, where they met their future wives. They both settled about a thirty-minute bus journey from each other.

'In our late twenties, we both began apprenticeships at an electricity power plant,' Stephen continued. 'Most weekends, we'd meet up for a bit of craic and a dance and a catch-up. Even for family occasions like baptisms and weddings, we were always there for each other.'

Stephen took a long pause before continuing his story. I noticed he'd gotten quiet, and I saw tears running down his face. Trying to compose himself, he asked me for a tissue.

'My life changed from being happy fifteen years ago, and I lost the will to live.'

He shared that on one Sunday morning, returning from Mass, he received a phone call from the power plant asking all employees to report for work. There had been a power failure affecting many homes that needed to be attended to immediately.

'Matt phoned me to say he was on his way in,' Stephen said, 'but I decided to delay going in myself for two hours. I'd promised my little grandson that I had a birthday gift for him.'

At twelve noon, while Stephen made his way to catch the bus to the power plant, he noticed a large traffic delay and was informed that all public transport on that route was cancelled due to an explosion at the plant.

Making his way home, he contacted the plant.

'I was told that there had been one fatality. They simply told me that it had been Matt. I crumbled after that phone call. All I wanted was to be beside my friend.'

Struggling with guilt and deep regret in the aftermath of the incident, Stephen retired five years later and returned to Ireland with his wife.

'I've always blamed myself,' he told me. 'I really felt like I had let Matt down, especially after making our promise many years ago.'

He talked of the subsequent years of withdrawing into himself, going from a man who had a great joy for life and family to not wanting to engage with life anymore. Through much sobbing, Stephen said that he had never allowed himself to talk of this for many years, being fearful that it might overwhelm him.

'I know I haven't forgiven myself for that morning, but I wonder if Matt ever forgave me for not being there to help him,' Stephen said softly.

Two hours later, we returned to Stephen's bedroom, where he requested to meet with a Catholic priest to receive the sacraments of Confession and Anointing. As Stephen sat on his bed, he looked over his glasses and let out a deep sigh.

'I have lived with this regret for many years and now I would like to leave it on this side of the grave,' he said simply. He was ready to let go, and that realisation did not overwhelm him.

Meeting with Stephen the following day, he revealed that he had made a request to his medical team.

'I would like to go home and be with my family for my final days,' he said. 'I'd like to spend more time with the grandchildren.'

A week later, one of our community palliative care nurses, Martina, let me know that Stephen had died in the company of his family. On the birthday of one of his grandchildren, as his family were enjoying a quiet but meaningful celebration, Stephen took his final breaths during the afternoon.

When we embrace and acknowledge our many fears, emotions and darkness as part of who we are, it gives that part less sway over us, because all it ever wants is to be acknowledged as part of our whole self. Our inner work is as real as our outer work and involves skills that anyone can develop, like journaling, reflective reading, spiritual direction, meditation and prayer. If we ignore our inner work, our outer life will suffer, just as it had with Stephen for far too many years.

Joe's Story

Joe was a gregarious man, with an effervescent personality. He was very much a people person, enjoying any and all conversations with people from all walks of life. With an abundance of silver hair and a neat moustache, he was a distinguished-looking man – I could see him sitting in the box of an opera house, fitting in very well.

It was morning time and while Joe was awaiting his morning coffee, he talked through his life story and his love of all things opera with me. *Madame Butterfly* was playing softly in the background in his room.

'Every opportunity we got, my wife and I visited all the opera houses we could get to,' he recalled. 'Italy, Eastern Europe – in recent years, they came to Dublin too, which saved on the air miles.

'I know the end is close,' he confided. 'I'm heading pretty quickly towards my demise, I fear, and I'm a little bit nervous in myself about it. I'm not sure what my final hours will be like, but I'm kind of hoping that when that time comes, I'll be more at peace.

Trying to tackle his sense of edginess, Joe also wondered if it was possible to have a haircut, and to access some chiropody, feeling that some action might distract him a little, and lessen that fear. Letting our volunteer hairdresser, Olive, know of Joe's request, she made him her priority that morning. It was heartening to observe her sensitivity and care of Joe as she trimmed his hair from his bedside, allowing him to be vulnerable, and engaging with him as if they were old friends. Later, Orla, our hospice chiropodist, arrived to attend to his podiatry needs. Martina, a healthcare assistant, shared his passion for opera, as they discussed the great opera houses of Europe that he loved to visit.

What Joe longed for, even at this time, was a little bit of normality, a distraction from his illness. All of these small actions allowed Joe to process what was going on for him, and in some way helped him to release his spiritual pain. When your anxiety levels decrease somewhat, it's easier to get a better sense of perspective of things.

Joe had the events of the morning to relate with enthusiasm to his family as they arrived early that afternoon. He died peacefully, in the company of his family, four days later. He had connected with his soul pain, and once all had been voiced, fear had lost its grip. We cared for Joe for six days, but he shared a whole lifetime with us.

I learned from Joe that it is good for all of us caregivers to be mindful that we are the medicine we bring. It is humbling to see what simple acts of courtesy can do. Doctor Michael Kearney, consultant in palliative medicine at Our Lady's Hospice in Dublin, acknowledges that if the dying person even begins to attend to their soul, the soul responds a thousandfold. Spiritual support is human involvement on the deepest level.

We live in two worlds: our inner world and our world outside. We need to find a bridge between both, through reflection and soul connection. We all need to offer ourselves good self-care, with an understanding that our inner world needs hospitality also. Each of us is a custodian of our inner world.

Kindness is a powerful medicine, and when offered with a generous heart, it has the power to heal our soul pain. Through the kindness of the hospice staff, Joe felt at ease to share his fears and concerns, and his spiritual pain around his approaching death.

In his recent Encyclical Letter, *Fratelli Tutti* [all brothers and sisters], Pope Francis tells us that:

> Kindness frees us from the cruelty that at times infects human relationships, from the anxiety that prevents us from thinking of others, from the frantic flurry of activity that forgets that others also have a right to

be happy. Often nowadays we find neither the time nor the energy to stop to be kind to others, to say 'excuse me', 'pardon me' or 'thank you'.

Yet every now and then, miraculously, a kind person appears and is willing to set everything else aside in order to show interest, to give the gift of a smile, to speak a word of encouragement, to listen amid general indifference. If we make a daily effort to do exactly this, we can create a healthy atmosphere in which misunderstandings can be overcome and conflict forestalled. Kindness ought to be cultivated; it is no superficial bourgeois virtue.

Precisely because it entails esteem and respect for others, once kindness becomes a culture within society it transforms lifestyles, relationships and the ways ideas are discussed and compared. Kindness facilitates the quest for consensus; it opens new paths where hostility and conflict would burn all bridges.

CHAPTER 2

Spiritual Medicine – A Third Branch of Medicine?

I've been thinking that perhaps it is time to look towards the development of a third branch of medicine, and call it spiritual medicine. I use this name to stress that in the work I do in hospice, I'm not dealing with conventional and psychiatric medicine, but rather working in the field of theology and pastoral work.

General and psychiatric medicine have not always existed as established sciences, but have developed through the centuries: medicine after the thirteenth century and especially in our time, and psychiatry throughout the last two centuries. I have learned through my pastoral work that the development of medical and psychiatric sciences raises new questions for theology and pastoral ministry, to look with new and fresh eyes at the need to support people suffering with spiritual pain. No wonder some have begun to consider and explore how spirituality and emotional health fit into a person's general wellbeing.

As human beings, we are made up of spirit, psyche and body. These aspects of the human person are mutually interdependent and cannot be healed or understood in isolation from one another. In his widely acclaimed publications around spiritual therapy, Croatian theologian Tomislav Ivančić tells us that everything that happens in a person's body and psyche, which they experience in the spirit, is manifested in their whole being. In a human being there are no separate spheres: for example, there is no illness which can be experienced only by an arm or a leg and not by the whole person. There is no such thing as a headache which affects only the head. A stomach operation is not limited only to the stomach. Following the same principle, a guilty conscience is experienced by the whole person, felt in the inner organs, on their skin and in their whole being, body, emotion and imagination.

In the past thirty years, there has been an increase in the number of theological and pastoral books written on the topic of spiritual therapy, all exploring faith and spiritual remedies for the healing of spiritual sickness. But at the same time, no one seems to identify spiritual suffering as illness.

When Dame Cicely Saunders established St Christopher's Hospice in London, she challenged the perception that people had to die in agony, advocating more understanding of the context of a patient's distress and looking for vital signs that consider not just the disease but the entire sick person. These signs might include anxiety and fear. Saunders encouraged doctors to expand their role as caregivers by asking their patients, 'How are you within?'

The impulse to distract ourselves in the face of sickness, by under-reporting symptoms or denying the seriousness of the illness, is indeed understandable. But we need to understand that spiritual pain is a normal part of living and dying, and for most of the time we have to just walk through it. As a chaplain I cannot offer a solution, but I can give patients and loved ones strength by listening. Listening means paying attention and having the desire to understand. That is a medicine in itself. Spiritual pain needs to be listened to and heard.

A good example of listening to spiritual pain is the process of childbirth. The pain can decrease as a mother relaxes into the birth when asked by the midwife to ride the waves of pain rather than fighting them. It is similar with emotional pain; leaning into the suffering can help the person to move through it. When we learn why the pain is trying to get our attention, we should do all in our power to acknowledge it.

Medical science confirms that emotional distress can and does increase a patient's physical symptoms. Stress can affect the body's immune system, slowing its natural capacity to heal. Exercises as simple as meditation or breath control can often give good relief.

Modern medicine is very effective in the medical management of pain and can control pain without compromising clarity of consciousness. This allows the patient time and space to address their concerns and fears. A passage from the ancient Buddhist text *The Tibetan Book of the*

Dead wisely stated, 'When the journey of my life has reached its end. And I wander through places of confusion. May I stay awake so as to transform fear and suffering.'

Susan's Story

Susan was in her late sixties when I met her. She was born in the UK to Irish parents, and was the ultimate English Rose, taking great care in her appearance. Her daughter Lydia married an Irishman and moved to East Galway, where Susan's much-adored four grandchildren were born.

Lydia and her then four-year-old son Finn had been involved in a serious car accident, resulting in Finn losing his left leg. With a long hospital stay in store for Finn, Susan decided to move to Ireland permanently, to be close with and have the support of her family. Finn, a resilient child, recovered well and eventually learned to walk with a prosthetic leg.

Five years after this move to Ireland, Susan received a diagnosis of an advanced cancer, which within a short time required hospice care. She was very open and emotional about her shock diagnosis, feeling it had come at a time that should be the best stage of her life. She was independent and enjoying her family in Ireland, yet was now faced with the realisation that the end of her life was approaching much sooner than she had expected.

Susan was bright and engaging, with an inner strength that was obvious in her daily approach to life: up early each morning, fully dressed for breakfast. She enjoyed having a routine in her day, whether she was attending physiotherapy with Deborah or art therapy with Ann. On occasion she'd take a mid-afternoon jacuzzi, a treat she enjoyed so much.

Susan was very creative and took some of her craft supplies with her to hospice, in the hope of completing some crochet and card projects. She was planning to give these as Christmas gifts to her grandchildren, and it became very clear that Susan felt a great emotional pain at the idea of not being around for all their special days through the years ahead.

One mid-December morning, when the festive atmosphere of Christmas was in the air and Christmas trees and decorations adorned the hospice corridors and dining room, I arrived at hospice early and received a message left by staff nurse Sorcha.

'Susan mentioned to me during the night that she would like to have a family get-together, maybe a Christmas fun day,' Sorcha explained. 'She's thinking especially of her grandchildren and she'd like to do an activity they could all enjoy together while she still has some energy.'

She had heard on local radio of an ice-skating rink close to the city and wondered if Finn, with his prosthetic leg, would be able to skate safely.

'I just want to have one final family get-together,' Susan explained when I spoke to her. 'I know it's Christmas time and I just want to have all of us together, to have some fun.'

We got the go-ahead for a visit to the ice rink from the medical team, who suggested having this family day sooner rather than later. That evening I drove to the skating rink, beautifully located overlooking the Claddagh area of Galway City. I remember lots of twinkling Christmas lights and music, as well as the laughter of young families having great fun. I met with the owner, John, and explained the situation to him, asking if it would be possible for Susan's grandson to skate safely.

He listened intently and pondered the request silently, before replying.

'This is what Christmas is all about: giving – giving to someone to be with their family for one last Christmas,' he said. John made a decision to close the ice-skating rink to the public on Thursday evening from 5 p.m. to 7 p.m. He asked the staff if they would be available to coach Susan and her family individually, to make it a special time for all. My heart rejoiced at the generous spirit of a man who chose goodwill over profit. What an example to his young staff.

We delivered the good news to Susan that evening, but she nonetheless lay awake for much of the night, reflecting on the reality that this was her final Christmas with her family. She acknowledged she was not ready to let go of life and family, feeling that there was so much more to live for, and too much to let go.

The following morning, she talked through her many fears and anxieties with me.

'I've decided to write a letter to each grandchild, to be opened on their next birthday,' she said. We then began to put a plan in place for their family outing to the ice-skating rink.

On Thursday afternoon, Susan and her family set off for the city in the family's people carrier, suitably dressed and with video camera firmly in hand. We were all so happy that this was happening for the family, but all felt a little anxious about how this fun-filled evening might turn out. We were concerned about falls, especially for Finn.

Three hours later, they all arrived back to hospice. I remember that everyone had been buoyed by the experience, but the children in particular were giddy with excitement. Susan was so delighted that she had set out on an adventure, and achieved it.

'The evening was beyond words,' she told us, smiling. 'It was the first time in months that I laughed from the heart. And Finn managed his skating so very well.'

She talked of the music, the Christmas lights, and the warmth of John and the staff. Her family joined Susan for a special evening tea at hospice before returning home. Their laughter and joy echoed through the corridors.

That night Susan slept well, feeling that something had shifted for her emotionally, a sense that she had completed a certain stage of life with her family. She described her experience as cathartic. Music and physical activity can and do help us process our emotions and there can be a release of emotional and spiritual pain as a result. For Susan, the outing to the ice rink with her family was her spiritual medicine, spreading a healing balm over her consciousness.

'Life isn't over yet,' she smiled. 'I still have some living to do. I'm going to make the best of these short weeks.'

The next day she made a decision to return home to be with her family for Santa's arrival on Christmas morning. Leaving hospice, Susan was tearful, knowing this could be the last time she saw us.

'I know I probably won't see you all again, but I'm most grateful,' she said. 'I found contentment again, pure and simple.'

Susan lived until the second day of the New Year, thankful to have had this special time with her family.

It's always good to remember, to paraphrase Austrian psychiatrist and Holocaust survivor

Viktor Frankl, that we may find meaning in life even when confronted with a hopeless situation. When facing a fate that cannot be changed, life has a meaning up to the last moment. When curing is no longer a possibility, there can still be healing. Untreated spiritual pain can escalate physical pain, and can in most cases lead to soul illness – hopelessness.

I sometimes describe spiritual pain as leaping out of your skin. No amount of pharmacological pain medication can numb or cure the inner turmoil of the person's deep distress. It is the role of the pastoral care professionals to discover and ask courageous questions that could help the sufferer identify their deepest spiritual wounds. Peace and healing are indeed possible only through soul work. It takes intuition, wisdom and courage to enquire what is going on beneath the surface of things. We are familiar with accessing the nature and degree of physical pain, and so I believe it is possible also, whether or not a person belongs to a faith or spiritual tradition, to ask Cicely Saunders's question: 'How are you within?'

Caroline's Story

With limited bed space and high demand, the number of days a person receives hospice care means that the time for addressing spiritual pain is also limited. However, I have on occasion advocated successfully through our medical director, Doctor Ita, the need for an extended admission time for a patient that I felt might reap good benefit from exploring and addressing their spiritual pain in greater measure.

Caroline was a day care hospice patient when I first met her. She had a very beautiful classical way of dressing, filled with colour, that reflected her personality. Caroline had always been energetic, and a woman constantly on the move, seeking adventure throughout her life. She was clearly a fan of the finer things in life, and loved her smoked salmon and artisanal chocolates, often breaking open a box and saying, 'Sit down there, Breda, and we'll have a nice chocolate.'

She was in her forties, and had been diagnosed with cancer two years earlier. Caroline was a journalist and worked in the editorial office of an Irish publication in the UK. She'd been born in the West of Ireland, and returned to her family home there as her disease progressed.

She was in and out of hospital a lot, and sadly had to endure news about the progression of her disease almost constantly. When a patient goes for a scan or test, there's always that 'in-between' time, when they're waiting for the results. There is often a feeling of anxiety and hope in that moment. More than anything, they don't want to hear that their physical condition has worsened. There is absolute delight when a person hears that their disease hasn't progressed. But if it has, their hopes are dashed anew.

'Can you believe that my life has come to this?' she asked me one day. 'I was happy and healthy, in a job that I loved. And now, I can't remember the last time I had a day where I did something that I enjoyed. I'm terrified.'

Caroline had a passion for the written and spoken word and had a beautiful flow of language, as she talked through her shock diagnosis of cancer in the prime of her life. She continued to write and kept a daily journal expressing her inner landscape, traversing her daily emotions of uncertainty and fear that now had become her unwelcome companions.

'All I can do now is simply write how I'm feeling,' she revealed. 'It helps, but it's also very scary.'

During our conversations, in an almost existential diagnosis of humanity, we explored many deep and fundamental questions together: where does existence come from? What is the purpose of this Earth? Who are we and where are we going? Where do we go after death?

'What is life all about?' she asked me one afternoon. 'What's the purpose of us being here?'

She turned her head away to rest her gaze on the artwork in the room. 'My soul hurts,' she admitted.

She felt that this was a pain that could not be reached or healed through conventional medication. However, she found comfort through spiritual language in her exploration of her Christian faith, a faith she had a renewed interest in during the course of her illness.

Caroline had begun to write poetry to express her inner turmoil and pain and found great healing through this expression. Through her writings, she was able to express the fear and anxiety she was feeling, to give expression to her long-held emotional and spiritual pain. She talked of her hope to have her work published eventually, but was realistic that her time was now short and this might not be possible.

Three days before Caroline's death, on a quiet afternoon, we both pored over her handwritten poetry. She pointed to a particular poem, called 'I Am the Drop'.

'This is my favourite,' she said, tapping the hardback notebook. 'This is me.'

'Caroline, would you like me to type up your poem and print it out for you?' I offered. When she agreed, I went to the office and typed up the poem, absorbing the truth in her words as I worked.

As she took the printed poem in her hands, her face lit up. 'Now I see what it might have looked like if it had been published,' she reflected.

We sat in companionable silence as Caroline looked over the words she had created.

'You know, I would like one day to write a book about my hospice experiences,' I confided in her. 'Should that happen, I would very much like to include your poem and your story.'

Her dream, it would seem, might have a life beyond this room.

'Yes, that would be lovely,' she smiled.

The following is Caroline's poem, dedicated to her memory and the great privilege of knowing her.

Breda Casserly

I Am the Drop
By Caroline Egan

I am the drop
that feeds the seed
of my emotion
Parched and sore
fertile and furtive
buried beneath the pastures of my heart.
I am the spring
that drenches over
bathes in bliss
and calls to life
my dormant desire.
I am the trickle
that tempers the toil
and draws from the bag
unloosens the coil.
I am the brook
that playfully flows
carries the rafts
of emotionless foes.
I am the tide
that once it's unleashed
will break down the dams
of dishonest disease.

I am the torrent that
turns to a flood
where trespassers waver
it's all understood.
And I am the drop that
drips night and day
a signature forming
its well in the clay.

What I really admired in Caroline was her deep tenacity. She believed in who she was, right through to the end. She had searched deep within herself and she'd found her own answers. Caroline gave herself time and space to reflect through writing and reading, and came to understand that life is a journey to be made. There's no real beginning and end, but there's a journey in between, and she tried as best as she could to bring life to that journey, through her renewed faith and her cathartic writing: her own forms of spiritual medicine.

In Susan and Caroline's stories we see that each of them found different paths to healing for their spiritual pain – one through expression of her feelings through writing and the other through the creation of memories to share with her family. Another path that people often turn to is religious spirituality, whether this is returning to a tradition they may have let go of years before, deepening a practice they have maintained throughout their lives, or discovering one that is entirely new to them.

Spiritual illnesses shows that the spirit has been damaged, and that it needs to be healed. Many people in today's world are in need of spiritual renewal, but people need a secure foundation from which they can begin to build this renewal.

Pope Francis tells us that the Church must be like a field hospital that cleans and heals wounds – 'So many people need their wounds healed. This is the mission of the Church: to heal the wounds of the heart, to open doors, to free people. To say that God forgives all.'

This offers encouragement and a big challenge to the Church to become conscious of itself and the riches it carries within, to begin to serve people more effectively and become more practical in its service, to come out from hidden corners and to step into the centre, where God has placed it.

Among the seven sacraments of the Catholic Church are Baptism and Confession which are believed to save the soul, and the Sacrament of Anointing which heals it. At the beginning of Mass we seek the forgiveness of sins, and before Holy Communion we ask for healing of our soul, 'Only say the word and my soul shall be healed'. The Church, through its pastoral work, should create in a person an experience of being surrounded by sympathy, forgiveness, trust and love, so that on this basis their soul can recover and be healed.

When we know that we were created out of love, we can freely enjoy life and know that death is only a passage to life, not the end of everything. God saved us by serving us. He wants to heal us. We were born to be loved and to love. Life is measured only by love. A person who lives in harmony with God does not experience themselves as a stranger to the world and indeed themselves, but feels welcomed into creation. Then our body and soul are friendly to ourselves, and the environment in which we live is friendly.

Walking with God, it becomes clear that we have a place and a purpose and we feel at home in everything we experience. As a person is not only body and soul but spirit as well, so our spirit finds deep joy and fulfilment in friendship with God. Being spiritually healthy means accepting and loving oneself. And in loving oneself, we love others also, we take care of our conscience in every respect, everything falls into place and everything has a meaning. Being spiritually healthy means avoiding conflict with our conscience, with truth, with values and with oneself. If we choose to live in harmony with ourselves, others, nature and God, our physical, mental and spiritual health should thrive. Then we just might become the person we were always meant to be.

Spiritual pain is a very real part of everyday life and of end of life too. And there are many paths to healing, to finding meaning and hope in the midst of dark and challenging times. A very important part of the work I do as chaplain is to explore spiritual pain with those experiencing it, to walk with them through this challenge, and to encourage them to find healing in whatever way they think will work best for them. This could be the simple act of talking about their pain and feeling heard and listened to. It could be prayer, or expression through creativity. Every patient is different, so their experience of spiritual pain will be different. And healing is available and open to all.

CHAPTER 3

Dealing with Life's Hurts – Forgiveness

Life has so many ways of teaching us what we most need to know but least want to hear about ourselves. Having the courage to look at what is happening in our lives can provide insight and material for great personal growth. Our outer reality can and does reflect our inner lives and can present many opportunities for us to learn and to grow. The landscape of our lives is a place where darkness and light, fear and joy, sadness and hope find a healthy balance within each of us.

Perhaps the most rewarding part of my ministry with patients is a life review exercise. This is an ancient practice, based loosely on the spiritual exercises of Saint Ignatius of Loyola. It's a very simple exercise, where I invite the patient to share their life story. I might say to them, 'Tell me a little bit about your life.' Most often, they are happy to share their life story, with a truth that goes deeper than opinions or ideas.

Looking back over a life that held great moments of celebration and wonderful achievements can bring comfort to a person, releasing a sense of gratitude for the many occasions that brought them happiness shared with family and friends. This life held joy and pain which shaped and moulded the person they have become. A life review can also give the patient clarity about unfinished business, in particular regarding their core relationships. They may face old fears, admit regrets, seek forgiveness, and in so doing complete their life's work. It is a way to clear the slate of the past, and results in a peace and a freedom that brings fresh meaning and wholeness to the person. This is a spiritual exercise that is worthwhile at any stage or age in life, not just at the end stage.

The area most often needing attention through a life review is forgiveness; most often, forgiveness of self, others and God. It is not easy, but the great benefit of forgiveness work is peace of mind and healing of the spirit. Forgiveness is key to good spiritual health and requires no special technique or experience except a willing heart and open spirit. However, a common barrier to forgiveness is a misunderstanding regarding what forgiveness is and is not.

Forgiveness does not mean forgetting, nor does it mean condoning or excusing offences. Forgiveness often goes against our natural instinct – we try to protect ourselves from further hurts, and so it requires a deliberate choice. Psychologists generally define forgiveness as a conscious, deliberate decision to release feelings of resentment or vengeance towards a person or group who has harmed you, regardless of whether they deserve your forgiveness. While there is some debate over whether true forgiveness requires positive feelings towards the offender, some agree that it at least involves letting go of deeply held negative feelings to bring the forgiver peace of mind and free them of corrosive anger, which does them no good whatsoever. Experts who study or teach forgiveness make clear that when you forgive, you do not gloss over or deny the seriousness of an offence against you. You are not obligated to reconcile with the person who harmed you, or release them from accountability.

Forgiveness is not something you offer to help the person who has hurt you; it is something you offer for your own wellbeing. This is such an important understanding to come to: by letting go through forgiveness, you are empowered to recognise the pain you suffered without letting that pain define you, enabling you to heal and move on with your life.

We will all be wronged to varying degrees throughout our lives, and for some of us, it might be something that has a lasting impact and leaves an indelible mark. Yet if we can learn how to forgive, and understand that by forgiving we are helping ourselves, we can move on from a deep hurt and live the life we deserve to live. Forgiveness is a process, and most forgiving is done gradually, allowing time and thought to create the space necessary to forgive. Initially, there is often anger or even rage. That usually softens into resentment and frustration. Finally, any lingering bitterness is replaced by a more mature balanced, objective perspective.

Many patients of religious practice can struggle with forgiveness of God – they are angry about the pain of their illness and the unfairness of their lives ending when they feel they have so much left they wish to do. They find it difficult to pray and grapple to find a new and different relationship with God. Sometimes patients can feel they are abandoned by God, and will ask 'Where is God in all of this?' However, the thought of being abandoned by God is very normal, even experienced by many saints. Faith without its doubts cannot grow. A crisis of faith is not a failure of faith, but a deep questioning, which is very healthy.

While others may need our forgiveness, and indeed we might need to forgive others, we may also need to forgive ourselves, perhaps for mistakes we have made, or times in our lives when we did not do right by others. And this may prove to be the most difficult task of all. It's also important to understand that forgiveness of others does not necessitate approaching the perpetrator; forgiveness can be done quietly in the heart. With this willingness to forgive others – in person or in our hearts – we free ourselves to live life well.

Jenny's Story

Jenny's admission to hospice was for pain management, and she was aware that her end of life was close. On our first meeting, I saw that Jenny was reserved, but with a warm personality – she talked at length about her physical pain and lack of sleep, but shared little about herself. Over the next couple of days, Jenny grew to trust my presence and began to share a little about her life. Jenny was sixty-four years of age, and had been diagnosed with cancer two years earlier. She was a retired professional, single, with no immediate family, but with good support from two close friends who were with her constantly, doing everything to support her from bringing her desserts to doing her laundry. They were friends who had taken time to be with Jenny, and they were friends she trusted.

Carole, the clinical nurse manager on duty, made me aware of Jenny's condition one morning; she had been in a lot of pain through the night and had been quite emotional and tearful.

When I entered her room, Jenny gestured to me to sit on the available chair. I entered with an open heart and willingness to hear what she had to say.

Jenny then began to sob uncontrollable tears. It took time for her to relax and find her voice.

'I'm very frightened – not of dying but of meeting God,' she finally blurted out. Jenny turned her head away as she talked through her many years of not being able to forgive God, her parents, but most of all herself. She was agitated and tearful as she shared her story of keeping a terrible secret for almost fifty years. I had a sense this was a private conversation, and not information that Jenny shared with many people, so I would rather leave the particular details of that conversation between the two of us. But I learned that Jenny had been through a very painful experience during her youth that she had been carrying with her ever since.

Deep anger surfaced as she talked of her now-deceased parents, who she said had 'good standing in the community'.

'My family were insistent, saying, "Don't let the neighbours know,"' Jenny told me. 'It was decided that it was for the best that we didn't talk about or explore this secret. I threw myself into my work, just to forget.'

She talked of putting it to the back of her mind as she went through college and began her career, but every now and again it surfaced and she tried hard not dwell on it. However, an experience in her late thirties brought the secret to light – another life chapter that I felt Jenny hadn't spoken about with many others – and she began to experience bouts of depression that affected both her personal and professional life. Her depression became so bad that she was admitted to hospital for a prolonged period of time. Jenny talked of living in a psychiatric hospital while working part time, and this became her way of living life for a number of years. Jenny's inability to forgive her parents made her relationship with them cold, to the point that she refused to see them. The comfort she found in prayer in her earlier years gave way to anger towards God. And most of all, she was haunted by her feelings of not being able to forgive herself.

Jenny talked of realising that since her diagnosis with cancer, she had lived a life of fear and anxiety in the shadow of a secret which dominated her thoughts. She had a sensitive nature and her distress about dying was escalated by a deep fear of meeting with God and how she might be judged. We explored together what might comfort her in relation to this fear and offer support in her desire to die peacefully.

A friend had given her a gift of a bible, which sat on her bedside locker. Jenny picked up the bible, and together we explored short passages that she requested I read aloud. I read this passage from the Prophet Isaiah (43): 'Because you are precious in my eyes, because you are honoured and I love you … Do not be afraid for I am with you.'

There was stillness and quiet in the room afterwards.

Jenny gestured that I stop, looked at me and asked, 'Do you believe that?' We explored together God's unconditional love for each person and His asking us to have no fear, that, He is with us. Jenny became tearful.

'I never allowed myself to be loved,' she reflected. 'I wonder what it might have been like if I had. How it might have changed things. Would things have been really different for me, I wonder?'

On my next meeting with Jenny, she requested to meet with a priest and receive the sacraments of Reconciliation and Anointing. Father Michael, our hospice-ordained chaplain, visited with Jenny and allowed her time to explore and receive the sacraments. Through the following two days,

Jenny talked of her funeral requests which she had put in place with the support of a friend. She had chosen cremation with the explanation, 'I want no trace of me to be left.' That moment still remains with me; it was one of the loneliest things I had ever heard anyone say.

Jenny particularly enjoyed visits from our aromatherapist, Martina, and our lunchtime volunteers who attended to her food requests – little treats that Jenny appreciated so much. Through subsequent conversations around death and afterlife, she asked if I could be with her at her moment of death and I assured Jenny if I was on duty and available, I would try as best I could.

As it happened, I was going past her room late one evening and knocked on her door. It was eleven days after her hospice admission. Inside, with Jenny, were her two good friends. They gestured to me to come in. Jenny was peaceful and taking her final breaths. I was grateful that I could fulfil Jenny's wish of being with her at the moment of her death.

At the end of her life, Jenny faced the secrets she had held deep within herself and was finally able to forgive herself and others, so that in the moment of death she felt at peace. I have no doubt that Jenny was greeted with deep compassion and love and great joy on the other side of the door.

Father Jim Cogley, a Catholic priest in the Diocese of Ferns in Ireland, tells us that secrets that are buried alive and issues that are swept under the carpet will inevitably wear through. Skeletons from the past will continue to draw attention to themselves in order to be given flesh. Past issues will always present until they are resolved and we view them in a different light and appreciate our learning from them.

How are we healed of our wounded memories? We are healed first of all by allowing them to be available, by inviting them out of the hidden darkness and by remembering them as part of our life stories. What is forgotten is unavailable, and what is unavailable cannot be healed. It is from this hidden place that they escape healing and can cause so much harm. We are the sum of all our past: we hear it in every crack!

In a poem he called 'Healing', D.H. Lawrence wrote:

I am not a mechanism, an assembly of various sections. And it is not because the mechanism is working wrongly, that I am

ill. I am ill because of wounds to the soul,
to the deep emotional self and the
wounds to the soul take a long, long time,
only time can help and patience, and a
certain difficult repentance long, difficult
repentance, realisation of life's mistake,
and the freeing oneself from endless
repetition of the mistake which mankind at
large has chosen to sanctify.

Forgiveness is a choice: of letting go and growing into the fully integrated, emotionally healthy person we are meant to be, offering ourselves compassion as we attend to our inner wounds. Forgiveness requires both strength and maturity, which is why Gandhi said, 'The weak can never forgive. Forgiveness is the attribute of the strong.'

Ruth and Alan's Story

Ruth's admission to hospice was very emotional for her husband and young family. Ruth had received a cancer diagnosis six months earlier and had not responded well to the subsequent treatments. She was aware that her time was short, with possibly only weeks of her life left. A woman in her early fifties, Ruth seemed to be very capable and confident. As she arrived with her husband, Alan, it quickly became clear that Ruth was the beating heart of the family.

'Part of you is thinking, "Do I have a future?" and is trying to absorb that reality, while the other part of you is aware of the immediacy of family life, and that children need to be picked up from school,' Ruth recalled of the moment she heard that her illness was terminal.

Alan was understandably in shock too, as were their three teenage children. Ruth was a very wise and practical young woman, realistic about her prognosis, and had great concern for her husband and children. It was evident that Ruth was a wonderful mother and homemaker. She talked at length about her emotional pain at having to leave her three teenage girls, and hoped that her husband would manage their upbringing well, with the support of extended family.

'I need to make plans and look to their future,' Ruth noted, referring to her children. 'I was looking through old family photos before I came here, and I realise how fast the years have gone and how they've grown so much. It's so painful to know I won't be there for exam results, the debs, first dates, their first broken heart.'

One afternoon while Ruth was resting, I joined Alan for a walk in the garden. He was understandably tearful as he tried to make sense of how their life had changed in such a short time and was trying to prepare himself and his daughters for what the next few weeks had in store for them.

'I can't believe it – she was so healthy,' Alan told me. 'Everything was going so well for us. I really expected life to be plain sailing. There was no reason in the world to think otherwise.'

He told me he was self-employed in a business that required a lot of his time, and had left much of the caring for family and home in Ruth's capable hands. His life plan was to work hard, retire possibly early in life, and then fully enjoy his family and some travel with Ruth. Alan had inherited his business from his parents who had instilled a firm ethic of hard work and achievement in him, their only child.

'In a family like mine, and with a background where everyone was strong and hardworking, the business is always important,' Alan admitted. 'You don't get to take a break from thinking about it. It becomes part of who you are.'

Alan felt he had to live up to his family's

expectations of continuing the business and the need to be successful. He talked of his many regrets of not being available for family occasions due to business commitments, his sense that he had spent more time at work than with family. And he was now experiencing feelings of regret about this which he was struggling with.

'I hope for the years ahead that I'll be a good dad to my children,' he reflected. 'I just hope I can live up to what Ruth wants for them. She always gave so much of herself to them.'

He wished life could be different. Ruth was the love of his life and now he was losing her. He felt there was so much he wanted to tell her – his deep love for her and his appreciation for her care of the family. He wanted to thank her for being such great support to him, but most of all, to talk about how he had always planned to be free to spend more time with his family in the future, and now he realised that family life without Ruth would never be the same.

He felt that as Ruth was receiving so many visitors, he found little time alone with her. We explored together the possibility of a visit to a local restaurant for them to have dinner together. Talking with staff nurse Bernie, we felt somewhere quiet with easy access might work, as Ruth's mobility was deteriorating. I contacted Glenlo Abbey Hotel, who in the past had facilitated a similar request for us. It was a five-star hotel, beautifully located overlooking the River Corrib, with distant views of the colourful Connemara landscape. They were most accommodating and happy to sponsor this request.

When I shared the details of the plan for their evening dinner at Glenlo Abbey with Ruth and Alan, both felt excited and were looking forward to the event. We decided on a Sunday evening at 6 p.m., requesting a window table, that they might enjoy the evening sunset over the River Corrib.

Ruth's sisters came in to help her dress fashionably for the evening and Alan and their three daughters arrived with a bouquet of roses. Both Ruth and Alan looked very much like a couple deeply in love as they left hospice that evening. There are many logistics involved in a night like this. At times, a nurse would accompany a patient for their social evening away from hospice. They would seat themselves at a respectful distance, to allow the family to enjoy the normality of an evening out. This support was not needed for Ruth.

Many hours later they arrived back; Ruth tired, but very happy to have had an evening with her husband. Alan stayed with Ruth at hospice that night.

The next day Alan and Ruth expressed their appreciation of their dinner out. While the evening was about having time alone together, it was much more than that – they had an opportunity to talk through their life together, to share what the future might hold for their three young daughters, with Alan making a decision to work less and to be available for the girls.

'We talked and sorted more in those two hours than we had done in our entire time together,' Ruth said later. 'It was an intimate evening, full of good chat that was real and deep. It allowed us the space to really talk about letting go.'

'More than anything I wanted to ask Ruth to forgive me for not taking responsibility for her and our children as I should have,' Alan added, with tears in his eyes.

Ruth felt that, though it was not her desire to leave her young daughters, she felt more at peace within herself having had the time to talk through her feelings and future for her family. They both agreed that the girls would be allowed to make their own decisions around future careers.

'I wish I'd had the courage to live a life true to myself, not the life others expected of me,' Alan said. 'This is a good lesson for me. I need to forgive myself for the times I put the needs of the business way ahead of the needs of Ruth and our children. I thought we would have many years ahead together; how wrong I was.'

Later that week we organised a movie evening in Ruth's room for Alan, Ruth and their three daughters. The girls chose to get pizza and screen the film *Casablanca*, a favourite of Ruth's.

'It was so special – sad but very special,' Ruth said afterwards. 'I'm not sure I even saw the film – I was so engrossed in loving them. I kept my girls close to me so that they could soak up all the love that I could give them for their lives ahead. It was a lovely memory for the girls, and I hope it will help them through their future.' I often observe this with patients for whom death is on its way. As Ruth did at this point, they live with an intensity and a beauty. There's often very little conversation left to be had, but the love in the room is tangible. All have come to a place of relative peace.

With the support of the hospice medical social workers, Ruth and Alan had many opportunities to talk to and be with their much-loved daughters. They spent time in the garden together, and even managed a short trip to the sea locally to savour the taste of ice-cream together.

Alan felt he had spent more time with Ruth and their girls through her hospice admission – almost four weeks – than he could remember in the past, and the business survived without his presence. He was grateful for this precious time together, and the awareness that work could continue successfully without him always at the helm.

Ruth requested the Sacrament of Anointing two days before her death, and asked for her family to be present. An inner journey had taken place; Ruth had found peace and was ready to let go.

In the weeks following Ruth's death, Alan's personal anguish about his regrets was never far from my thinking. It reminded me of some of my own regrets in life, and how I had to learn how to practise self-compassion.

When I was nine years old, I was diagnosed with scoliosis, a curvature of the spine, which meant that I had to wear a brace to support my spine as I grew. Perhaps understandably, I was told that, owing to my condition, I was exempt from classroom chores. To other children, this may have been a delight, but for me, it only gave me a heightened sense of feeling different from everyone else. It gave me a need to become the best at everything I possibly could be: the best cyclist, the best at handwriting, the best in the class at maths.

A few years later, I entered a nationwide storytelling competition. The announcement of winners came on the radio, and I heard my name as they announced who had placed third. For other children, placing third in the country would have been a great achievement, but for me, I felt the disappointment of failure; that I just wasn't good enough.

I set very high standards; not necessarily to please myself, but to show the wider world what I could achieve. As I moved through my career as an adult, the need to prove myself and be the best was always there.

I did not practise good self-care through the years of setting up the business in handmade chocolates. I truly believed that achievement was only possible through long hours of hard work. I worked constantly, six days a week, with little time to rest. I seldom took time off. My own personal needs drifted into the background.

Around this time, I went for a routine smear test, and the results showed pre-cancerous cells. This started a time of treatments and surgery, but also forced me to take a serious look at how I was living my life.

It was painful to realise that I hadn't considered my own personal needs for so long. This was the point where I began to review my life and slowly begin to become a bit more self-aware. I realised I needed to show some kindness and respect for myself. I had pushed myself to a point of near exhaustion.

I took some time away from the chocolate business to reflect on my own needs and came to the realisation I was quite exhausted. I gave myself space to be nurtured by nature and to spend time in quiet and peace, and to listen deeply to my own needs.

I remembered the little child who fought so hard to be recognised in the classroom, to be the best. I came to understand that my striving in life, although well-intentioned, was draining me of all energy. In a sense the business had taken over my life. I had little time for a social or personal life. As painful as it was, I needed to forgive myself for the many times I didn't listen to what my real need was. Just to be Breda.

It is possible to ease a sorrow and to smooth out difficulties with honesty and, above all, a great deal of love. And sometimes we need to send that love towards ourselves. We need to live at soul level, with reflective, gracious living. When someone realises that their life is now limited, they live with a new determination – to share the story of their lives with others.

We all have a dark or shadow side, a place where our wounded selves live. It's the place that holds our unresolved issues, a place that is always looking for our attention, but sadly, the part of ourselves we are most likely to reject. However, when we grow to accept this part of ourselves, to accept what is not perfect in us, we might just grow to be fully human.

Our journey to maturity and self-compassion is indeed paradoxical. We mostly grow by falling apart; accepting that at times we are vulnerable, fragile, imperfect human beings. Being self-aware, and integrating our dark or shadow side, is a lifelong journey. Very often, we learn the greatest truths about ourselves through the mistakes we made and the wrong turns we took in life. It takes a lifetime to grow into the person we were born to be,

Through reflection, and awareness that time is short, the dying often have a clear sense of what needs to be done. They sense that life is ebbing away, and they might like to put something to rest. It's often a simple thing like not having spent enough time with the family. Others talk about not living the life they'd wanted to live, or occasionally, not making something of their lives.

But often, a life review is simply about looking back over a life that held great moments of celebration and wonderful achievements. There's a sense of gratitude for the many occasions that brought happiness. Clearing the slate of the past results in a peace and a freedom that brings fresh meaning and wholeness to the person. And this can encourage those around them to do the same.

CHAPTER 4

Just Be You

People can be so busy building a career and life around them that they often forget to sit and ask themselves some fundamental questions: 'Is this really the life that I want? Am I content with the life I've chosen to live? Whose standards am I living up to? Are they standards imposed by the world around me, or my own? What choices have I made in living my life? Who am I living my life for?'

Some people do take a step back and take stock of their lives, asking themselves whether or not they're living their life according to their values and who they truly want to be; questioning how they have been living and what they may wish to change. Sometimes this 'check-in' is a natural decision, an instinct, but more often this is caused by an unexpected challenge, such as burnout or mental health struggles, physical illness or the loss of a loved one.

When we're challenged in life through illness or some other major catastrophe, our soul is asking us to take the simple task of doing a life review. We have spoken previously about life reviews in the context of people who are reaching the end of their lives due to illness and are now looking back, but in this instance a life review is more about asking these questions about how we are living our lives now.

Maybe this isn't the life for you. Maybe you're not being true to your authentic self. It can be difficult, but taking the time to reflect through these times can yield great results.

Living a life untrue to your deep nature can present untold stresses and deep soul pain. However, life on a road with scenery and a pace that suits your nature can result in a quality of life that brings deep satisfaction.

A good piece of advice from American philosopher Ralph Waldo Emerson tells us that 'To be yourself in a world that is constantly trying to make you something else is the greatest accomplishment.' Only those who are in touch with themselves and their own peculiarities can be friendly and mindful to others. Because the person we know best is ourselves. And you stay with that person who you know really well – and hopefully like – in good times and in bad.

We must trust ourselves to build the life we want. In the face of all adversity, we must choose our attitude. While trying to be true to yourself, and live the life you want, you have to face the fact that change will happen. Being true to who you are has little to do with your success or your status, but has everything to do with your character. Along with attitude, your character is all about what choices you make rather than what happens to you. As we mature and grow in greater self-awareness, we experience more freedom to be the real us.

We all have an inner voice that encourages each of us to pursue our dreams, no matter what the cost; to take risks, to live life to the fullest. However, there are other voices, outside as well as within, and they shout different messages, often in disagreement. They tell us to play it safe and be the same as everyone else. 'What if we fail?' they ask. 'What if others do not like it and I end up being rejected?' The inner voice, beneath any fear or worries we might be experiencing, belongs to our soul, as it encourages us to pursue our destiny. So each time we play the game of conforming, our inner voice will continue to shout louder. All other voices are probably well-intentioned, and very often come from a place of love and concern, even the voice of experience. Yet while they represent the good in our lives, they fall short of the best. The cost of ignoring our soul's voice, and refusing to honour our own drumbeat, is to condemn ourselves to frustration and mediocrity. Learning to listen to this voice and prioritise it over the others is a lesson that can take a long time to learn, but it is always worth it in the end, as this will help set us on the road to happiness.

Sean's Story

Doctor Ita referred me to Sean, a man in his late sixties, feeling that he might benefit from spiritual support. His admission to hospice was for symptom control, but we were keenly aware that the admission may progress to end-of-life care.

When I first met Sean, he was curled up on his bed with the bedclothes up to his nose, staring absently into the distance. Slightly dishevelled and quite thin, Sean's frightened demeanour was striking. I got the impression he was a man who was used to turning his back on the world.

In a hospice environment, there is a full multidisciplinary team, and within the first two days of admission for a patient, we all introduce ourselves and identify our roles: doctor, nurse, consultant, healthcare assistant, chaplain, art therapists, occupational therapists, physical therapists, etc. For some patients, seeing all these new faces can be very overwhelming, especially given how vulnerable a mindset they are already in. Very often, it helps to assure them: 'You don't have to remember all our names. You'll get used to all of us through the days ahead. It's more important for us that *we* remember *your* name.'

I noticed that Sean found it difficult to unpack and settle; the clothes were flung on top of his suitcase, while his coat hung by the door. My sense was that he was a restless spirit, who didn't intend to stay in hospice for long.

'I'm tired. Frustrated," he told me when I went into his room and greeted him that day. 'I don't have the energy to get out of bed today.'

'Is there anything we can do to help you, Sean?'

'I just want to be on my own.'

As I left his bedspace, I turned towards him. 'Sean, I'm around at any time if you need to have a chat.' He responded by pulling the bedclothes around him tighter.

To allow Sean time to settle into the hospice environment, I waited a couple of days before I returned to him. He was a little brighter, though still defensive in his conversation and somewhat angry with life and the world generally.

'How are you today, Sean?'

'Fine.'

'Would you like to go and get some fresh air today?'

'No.'

And then, after a pause, he admitted: 'There's nothing left for me in life.'

I sensed a deep vulnerability in Sean – he was almost like a fledgling bird that was frightened and trapped and had no way of escaping. He seemed quite restless, looking out the window a lot.

Over the next six weeks, I spent a lot of time with Sean. He was challenging and difficult at times, as he expressed his frustration in colourful words. He had no problem telling you to go away and leave him alone. He wasn't used to a hospice environment, and he rebelled against it. His only way of dealing with that fear was to express himself with angry language.

One evening, as the nurse came to his bedspace with his medication, Sean sent the pills flying all over the floor with one swoop of his hand.

'I don't want to take any of that,' he insisted.

Beyond his daily façade of non-compliance, I came to realise there was a deeply wounded human person, who gave expression to his soul pain by being angry and aggressive with everyone around him.

'I'm just not happy here,' he'd say, over and over.

I gently encouraged Sean to share his life story, allowing him time and space to bring his emotional pain to a level where it could be shared. I offered him support to make sense of his many difficult life experiences, encouraging him to perhaps view them in other ways.

'What was life like growing up for you, Sean?' I asked.

Sean told me that he had emigrated from a small Irish-speaking village to the UK at sixteen years of age.

'Sure I was only a young lad when I had to take the train and boat to England,' he recalled. 'All I had was a few words of the English language. There was nothing for me at home. To be honest, the city swallowed me right up. It was fairly frightening.'

As he had no trade or skill, he depended daily on finding construction work. With poor accommodation and few friends, he found solace and comfort in the Irish pubs.

'All I had in the evenings was to go to the Irish pub and stay there until closing time,' he revealed. 'And I got a bit too fond of the drink.'

Sean was married in his early twenties, had three children and separated from his family in his thirties. Over the coming weeks Sean talked of his sense of displacement, having to leave his childhood home so young, with no life experience. He also talked of the deep loneliness and guilt of being separated from his now-adult children.

He recalled his depth of loneliness for the

small family farm, the sea and a culture that had nourished him emotionally.

'I felt so at home in my own little village in the West of Ireland, working out in the fields, and doing a bit of fishing,' he said fondly. 'It was where my family were. That was the life I loved, and looking back, probably should have stayed with.'

Sean talked of feeling less than human, his self-hatred, and above all his childhood dreams of making a life for himself close to the sea, in a land that offered him so much freedom in his youth. He was heartbroken being separated from his true nature and what he had felt would have made him happy.

'There were times I lived on the streets,' he revealed. 'I couldn't believe who I had become. It was not the life I'd hoped for. When I was a young lad I had dreamed of a better life, like everyone else in my village. We went abroad to make something of ourselves. But it didn't always turn out like that.'

Sean then spoke of his lowest point. 'One night I was cold and wet on the streets. I was hungry and tired, with no friendly face around, and I thought of my little village at home. All I could do was dream about the open land and sea. It was all that kept me going.'

Through many winter afternoons, Sean and I sat in the conservatory alongside his bedspace, with mugs of tea. We would talk, but more often than not we shared a comfortable silence. His aggressive and angry behaviour gave way to a human vulnerability that held such beauty.

He began to share old stories and sing old songs from his childhood village that still held his heart. A picture soon emerged of a tightly knit, seafaring village where people liked to visit each other's homes in the long winter evenings and trade traditional tales. You can only imagine the chasm between that life and the chaotic buzz of an industrial city in the UK. One song he loved in particular was 'Óró mo Bháidín', a typical Connemara song. He talked about what was the best part of his life, which was his youth.

'If I had my life over again, I wouldn't leave,' he reflected one day. 'I'd stay at home with my own people.'

Sean had eventually realised his dream to return to the West of Ireland, although he only got to enjoy that life for a short time, before his cancer diagnosis. He could now in some small measure face himself, and had an awareness that he had unconsciously projected his own hurts onto others through the years. Sean had made a journey home to the heart of himself.

As Sean deteriorated, he was moved to a quiet single room, overlooking the hospice winter garden, where he particularly enjoyed looking out at the lush greenness outside his window.

'And beyond that, Sean, lies the sea,' I reminded him.

'The sea,' he echoed. A look passed over his face; one where he was beginning to look more at home within himself.

His daughter Michelle had made contact and began to visit her father before his death. They hadn't met for almost ten years. Their interactions were polite and quietly reserved to begin with, but Michelle soon became more relaxed in the hospice environment, and at her father's bedside.

Conversations between the pair eventually turned to family. Things stayed light, but it was clearly very emotional for them both, and many tears were shed. In some ways, Michelle had now become the parent. Sean was almost shy around her, but very happy, and so grateful that she'd made contact with him. He drew great comfort from it in his final days.

On the day he died, I sat with Sean quietly in the morning as he awaited his daughter. The stillness in his body and the sense of comfort around him indicated that he was finally at peace.

By the time Michelle arrived, Sean was lying comfortably in his bed, unresponsive. She gladly took his hand, still talking with him.

His elderly, frail and unwell mother telephoned the hospice. She had been aware of Sean's condition, and it broke her heart that she was not mobile and unable to be with him. Emotionally, she made one request – her final act of love for her son.

'Would you make sure that Sean receives the Sacrament of Anointing?' she asked.

Sean was now quiet as he approached his final moments of life with Michelle beside him.

Later, a few hours after Sean had passed away, Michelle asked to speak to me.

'Before I go, I wanted to thank you all for looking after my dad,' she said. 'I know he could be difficult at times, so I just hope that he didn't upset any of you too much.'

As I listened to Michelle, I could sense her love and protection for her dad, a man from whom she was estranged for many years, but in recent days had bonded deeply with. She had also found a measure of healing.

'But, you know, he never means it,' she continued. 'Underneath it all, he was a kind man.' She paused, and then added: 'I'm really sorry I didn't have more time to get to know him.'

She had encountered a different father in Sean's final days. She had found a man who was kind and fatherly. A father who had had a proper conversation with her, probably for the first time in her life. Most significantly, she had seen a father who was finally able to say he was sorry. I felt very strongly that Sean was able to have this experience of getting to know his daughter because he had finally known himself and given to himself what he felt would make him happy – first, a return home, and then being able to express his feelings about his past, his family and himself with honesty and vulnerability.

As we talked, I recalled my initial impression of Sean and how that changed as I got to know him, and he got to know himself better. 'Well,

Sean became a great teacher for me,' I told her. 'He nurtured deep empathy and compassion within me.'

I read the questioning look on Michelle's face.

'He challenged me to reflect on my own thinking,' I continued. 'He confronted me with the thought that not all people fit into a conventional narrative. For this lesson, I am most grateful.'

Just as it happened to Sean, with each patient we witness a struggle to cope with their new identity – a humanity stripped of all non-essentials. It is especially then that they become our teachers in the human skills necessary for our caring roles.

I have come to understand that even in the darkest recesses of life, some hope will be found and light will always break through, if not to banish the dark, then at least to light the path through it. And so in hospice the excellent clinical care is offered together with a vigilance of the heart, attentive to the small things that make all the difference.

In order to grow into the person we are meant to be, there is a fundamental question we need to ask ourselves: when the harshness of life strips me of many of the things that I value, how do I live so I do not remain closed to the wisdom offered by this experience, so that I am not destroyed? For there is no denying it – the heart breaks in different ways. It can break in a way that softens and opens it in compassion and selflessness. Or it can break in a way that makes it hard, cold and closed. The pains of life and the losses we undergo are either transmitted or transformed. If they are not transformed through acknowledgement and a measure of acceptance, we transmit them outwards, causing the pain and hurt to flow into our attitudes and relationships. It comes out in behaviours like hypersensitivity, sarcasm, anger, resentment, living in the past, being critical of anything new and using words that wound and pull down. Hurt people tend to hurt people; life shapes us. How do we respond? There is a learning and wisdom in all experiences. That's growth. Getting to know oneself is an ongoing process, because we are changing all the time as we make our way through life. Something that may have been true about us at one time doesn't always remain true, but often the essence of us remains the same. And opening ourselves up to change and to vulnerability helps us to learn the most about ourselves, even though this isn't always easy.

The thirteenth-century Persian poet Rumi offers great insight into the vulnerability and fragility of the human person, while encouraging us to accept with gratitude the richness of our inner world, in his poem 'The Guest House':

This being human is a guest house.
Every morning a new arrival.
A joy, a depression, a meanness,
some momentary awareness comes
as an unexpected visitor.
Welcome and entertain them all!
Even if they are a crowd of sorrows,
who violently sweep your house
empty of its furniture,
still, treat each guest honourably.
He may be clearing you out
for some new delight.
The dark thought, the shame, the malice,
meet them at the door laughing
and invite them in.
Be grateful for whatever comes,
because each has been sent
as a guide from beyond.

Dan's Story

Early one Wednesday morning, Carol, one of our hospice day care nurses, dropped into the pastoral care office, enquiring if I had some time that morning to meet with Dan, who was seventy-four. His doctor had rightly deduced that he now needed hospice medical care, so he had referred Dan to our day care hospice services, for one day each week.

Carol shared that Dan appeared to be very much alone in himself, not engaging with other patients or indeed nursing staff.

Dan lived alone in a fairly remote part of the countryside. Seated in an armchair in a corner of the day care room, with life bustling all around him – patients planning their visit to the hairdresser, aromatherapist, physiotherapist, art therapy or flower arranging, along with their medical and nursing needs – Dan looked quite lost and alone. He was a man used to caring for himself and had his own daily routine at home.

When I approached him, I noticed that he was a very shy man. His body language seemed closed, and his head was down.

'Dan, you're new to us here at hospice, and you're very welcome,' I told him, by way of greeting.

'Grand, grand,' he nodded.

'It takes a while to get used to a new place, Dan, doesn't it?' I began, trying to make him feel at ease.

'Oh it does. It takes a long time.'

Enquiring if he would like a walk in the garden, Dan was on his feet before I finished the sentence. He talked little and appeared sad and ill at ease in himself.

For the next six weeks I met Dan each Wednesday. Very slowly he came to trust my presence, as we shared an interest in travel and the natural world.

As he talked about the shrubs and flowers – he knew the name of every plant and flower in the garden – I saw light in his face and he started to open up.

'What did you work at?' I asked him.

'I worked as a long-distance truck driver, from Ireland through many European countries, delivering non-perishable goods,' he explained. 'I liked the freedom. I liked being out and about. You'd meet all walks of life in that job.'

'How are things at home, Dan?' I asked him.

'Fine, fine,' he said quickly.

He gave away little of his personal life, shying away from the conversation as it arose through the weeks. On that, he didn't seem to want to elaborate at all.

On one particular Wednesday, Dan became unwell in day care and was admitted to our hospice Inpatient Unit. It was a short stay of one week, but a week that allowed Dan to experience hospice care differently, in a quiet and gentle way. He settled well, enjoying listening to the radio and engaging in banter with healthcare assistants Gerry and Simon. In fact, he began to really blossom through this week.

Dan began to share his vulnerability slowly through talking about his life story. For the next three months, Dan and myself met regularly as he returned to day dare. He was quite measured in his sharing in the beginning, but from week to week his story unfolded with authenticity and honesty.

'Growing up in a family of four on a small farm, life was not easy,' he said. 'I was only eight when my mother died. She wasn't sick for long, and I was never told what had happened to her. After that, the house became quiet.'

Trying to manage home and farm, his father withdrew into himself, and often took the children away from school to work on the farm. Dan then became emotional as he talked of his schooldays.

'They were a very bad experience for me,' he admitted. 'On the days I could attend school, one teacher regularly made a laughing stock of me. He knew that I couldn't read well, because of my poor attendance, but he would call me to the front of the class to read the lesson anyway. The class would often laugh at me. I found that very painful. I would go home and sit in the house for hours being upset about it.'

When he was eleven, Dan left school, just about able to read and write. For a number of years he worked on the family farm and with other local farmers when he could find work.

'I'd come home to a cold, dark house, and would always be hungry,' he recalled. 'More than anything, I was lonesome for my mother.'

He described himself as 'odd', not wanting to mix with other people. In his late teens Dan learned to drive, and enjoyed this experience very much. He worked with a local creamery, collecting milk from local farmers to be taken there for processing.

In his thirties, Dan found employment with a small haulage company, delivering goods throughout Ireland – long hours, but he enjoyed the travel.

'The only big comfort in life in those days was to go to the pub,' Dan told me. 'At least there was a bit of heat there, and other people. The sport on the TV was a bit of a bonus.'

As the haulage company expanded, Dan began to travel more to European countries, saying that although his poor literacy skills challenged him through those years, he managed reasonably well. Through the weeks of sharing his life story, Dan would often refer back to his schooldays and the teacher who he felt had destroyed his confidence at a young and vulnerable stage of his life. He mentioned this teacher time and time again.

Dan's final admission to hospice was for end-of-life care. One week later it was his seventy-fifth birthday. He had grown to feel comfortable with the staff and we surprised him with a birthday cake brightly adorned with candles. Dan was visibly delighted.

'It's the first time I ever remember hearing anyone sing 'Happy Birthday' for me,' he told us. Afterwards, we reflected as a team on just how incredibly sad this was. The moment was an awakening for us, too. He later told us that his two years of illness were, in a strange way, the best years of his life. He had experienced the goodness and kindness of others that he hadn't felt throughout his life. Yet Dan had also reflected that, due to that childhood trauma, he had not developed or grown as a person in the way he might have wanted. He felt he hadn't had the opportunity to connect with people, to open himself up to them, and to really be himself around them.

'I really didn't get to live life at all,' he reflected one evening. 'I'm seventy-five, but sometimes I think I never really lived past thirty.' He had shunned life and people, and felt loneliness deeply.

'Dan, is there anything you really enjoyed in life?' I asked him.

His face lit up. He knew exactly what to say to this question.

'I loved to grow roses,' he said. 'I was good at it, too. My mother was gifted at it, so I must have taken it from her.'

We talked of the roses that grew in the hospice garden, and with great enthusiasm, he shared the names and best soil for certain rose beds. He talked of one particular rose bush that would thrive in the West of Ireland soil.

'I like to grow roses too, Dan,' I told him. 'Would you recommend one that might grow well in the soil close to the sea?'

'My favourite rose is a very hardy type,' he said fondly. 'You can get it to thrive in almost any condition.'

'Well if you don't mind, Dan, I'd like to plant this rose in my own garden, to remember you,' I told him.

Tears welled up in his eyes. 'That means a lot to me,' he whispered.

Dan died alone and quietly in his sleep, a man who lived unknown to almost everyone, but had touched our hearts deeply.

I did get to plant Dan's rose bush in my home garden. It was such an obscure and old variety of rose that many of the staff in the garden centres I visited to enquire about it were stumped and impressed in equal measure.

'Wow, you must be some kind of genius if you know about that variety of rose,' one staff member noted.

'I had a good mentor,' I told him.

Each June, as the pink roses bloom in abundance, and are admired by all who pass by, I quietly smile and think of Dan.

I think all of us in life can pinpoint a moment where we are forced to be true to ourselves, even in the face of overwhelming evidence that suggests a different path.

In my thirties, I became engaged to be married to Joseph, a very kind and good man. We had enjoyed each other's company a lot, often bonding through our shared love of the great outdoors.

His proposal came out of the blue, although he admitted that he had been planning this moment for some time. It was a happy surprise, and I gladly accepted. Yet in the ensuing weeks, I couldn't shake a deep, visceral feeling that this marriage was not for me. There was no reason for this other than a gut instinct. It was painful to plan a future with the realisation that it really wasn't what I wanted. This small, but clear inner voice was simply saying, 'No.'

Joseph picked up on my apprehension quite well. He had been talking about the future more than I had, and had sensed my lack of energy around the subject.

'Is there something wrong, Breda?' he said finally. 'I have a sense that something might be.'

'I find it very difficult to explain this to you, but it's just a sense that I have,' I said. 'This has absolutely nothing to do with you. You're one of the nicest people I've ever met, but I have this deep, deep instinct that marriage is not for me.'

It's truly difficult to explain to someone who is planning their entire future around you that your only reason to not join them on that journey is 'gut instinct'. There were, needless to say, lots of tears.

Although this instinct was strong, I still found this time emotionally dark and painful. It was distressing, too, to see Joseph, this very kind man, coming to terms with what was clearly a very painful experience. On occasion, I thought it might have been easier to go ahead and get married, but in the end I really do believe the decision I made was the right one, for both of us.

I listened to my own small inner voice, despite the well-intentioned advice from many friends that urged to me go ahead and get married. 'It's just pre-wedding nerves,' they would say.

To be honest, there are occasional times when I might think, 'What if?', but the truth is that I've never regretted this decision. By getting married, I believe I would have lost the most rewarding and growth-filled years I've had as a healthcare chaplain. It was a lonely road at the time, but I can say with surety that I was on the road that allowed me to be true to myself.

Most often, we view life through the lens of our past experiences and if this view is painful and has wounded our spirit, then we seek a journey of healing and wholeness. Our past does not have to define our future.

There comes a time when we need to be present to ourselves and our feelings – to be accepting of ourselves. This can be very challenging in a judgemental culture. It is only when we are emptied of the false self, and feel secure in ourselves, that we can reach out to others who will sense that they too are being offered permission to be their authentic selves. It is like what flight attendants say in their safety messages on airplanes about applying your own oxygen mask before helping others with theirs. The stronger you are in your self-belief, the more you are able to live according to your own truth, the more able you will feel to reach out to others with generosity and compassion, and live a life you will look back on later with comfort and peace.

CHAPTER 5

The Importance of Storytelling

Story is important for those who are dying because it validates their freedom to conclude their own story. No matter how close one is to death it is never too late to claim authorship of one's life. Stories told by the dying are privileged acts of self-interpretation; they are the final stories they tell. These are stories told by people who have a particular awareness of their mortality and told in an effort to make sense of their world.

A person's story is the frame through which they view their lives. When a dying person tells their story, it creates a sense of meaning around what they have experienced, which is a fundamental human need and important for resilience. And this sharing of their story can reduce stress, clarify thought and help them to better communicate with others.

Storytelling and ritual-making are not merely something that humans do; they are essential as we navigate our way through our lives. Together they enable us to create a world that is both habitable and hospitable; they are also the fundamental means for shaping and sustaining our journey into the Divine (death). The great mystery of death and the grief and sorrow that attend it require rituals of storytelling and remembering.

When you hear a story, you leave your own reality and place yourself in someone else's shoes. You get to experience their life, to engage in their emotions and actions. A good story can draw us in and fire our imaginations. It can also tap into our deepest feelings and help us to see life in a new and profound way.

Humans are empathetic creatures. And as such, we respond to stories because they cultivate emotion and a sense of togetherness –

a connection. Stories make us feel like part of something bigger than ourselves. Story is leading to a singular goal, and ideally confirming some truth that deepens our understanding of who we are as human beings.

Tara's Story

As hospice staff, although we are very much aware that death does not come for us only in our older years, there is still an acute sense of shock and sadness when we hear of the admission of a young patient. The sadness is even more heightened when it is a young parent.

As a chaplain, I have no answers for these young patients. One feels most inadequate in a situation like this. I feel challenged by the sense of unfairness that has been presented to their family. Standing outside the door of their room, so many emotions bubble up within me, and I have to take a deep breath before I knock.

I often wonder, how will I be received as a chaplain? Understandably, the patient can be feeling a lot of anger, and if the anger is towards God, that can sometimes be projected onto the chaplain that stands before them. Though this is difficult, I can accept it fully and can see beyond the anger to the human person, struggling with all their might to hold onto life.

What met me on the other side of the door one afternoon took me by such surprise. Inside the room was a young woman with dark, expressive eyes and a bright, vivacious demeanour. By the window, an older woman sat, seeming much more reserved.

'Oh, you're the chaplain! And a woman! Brilliant. Come sit with me,' the young woman said.

Tara, thirty-five, was married to George, and they had a six-year-old son, Luke.

She looked younger than her years, was dressed in vibrant colours and put me at ease immediately. She introduced me to her mother – the quiet lady sitting and observing us from the window.

Tara cut through all of the life conversations and went straight to talking about her existential pain. This was something she shared, surprisingly, with great ease and comfort.

She pointed to her head. 'I haven't a screed of hair, the effects of chemotherapy,' she told me, seemingly very at home in her own skin.

'You know, Breda, I love life,' she admitted.

'Life has been very good to me.' I could hear in her voice her joie de vivre. She'd had an interesting and adventurous life, full of travel and backpacking and people who were utterly charmed by her everywhere that she went.

She had been approached by a talent agent on a visit to London with some friends but instead of the cut and thrust of a big city, she'd wanted to move west, where she loved the rugged landscape. And before her diagnosis, she had been looking forward to seeing her young son grow up there.

She held her phone in her hand, where she'd been looking at photographs; it was clear that her family – her son in particular – were rarely far from her mind.

'There's one thing bothering me,' Tara continued. 'I want to talk about what's going to happen, but my family keep changing the subject on me.' She looked towards her mother, hoping that this one time she might acquiesce and have this terrible conversation that her daughter so badly needed.

On hearing this, however, Tara's mother picked up her handbag. 'I'll leave you to it, so,' she said, making her way towards the door.

'Mum,' Tara said beseechingly. 'Please come and sit with us.'

After a moment of hesitation, Tara's mother pulled up her chair. Tara extended her hand so that the two could hold hands.

'I want to talk about it. I need you to talk with me,' she said tearfully to her mother. 'I know you're only trying to protect me, but I need to talk, I know my time is short, I know I'm going to die, and I need for all of us to be able to talk. Properly. I know this is hard, but it's really important for me, Mum.'

Her mother, exhaustion etched all over her face and body, took her young daughter's face in her hands. 'It's so painful for me, Tara,' she replied, her voice cracking. 'You're my daughter. You shouldn't have to go through any of this, and I just want to protect you. If I could take your place, don't you know I'd gladly do it.'

Tara longed to share this need to tell her story with the people she loved, especially with her sisters, and felt that her life in some way would be incomplete without those real, authentic and important conversations. Very often, a patient really longs for their family to talk about the realities of what is going on for them, and what will happen as they die. For the most part, families have much more difficulty with this moment than the patient.

I listened quietly as Tara and her mother tentatively broke open the conversation. After a few moments and plenty of tears, the honesty finally tumbled out. They shared some happy memories: about growing up, family birthdays and family holidays enjoyed together. But they also spoke about their fears and their grief, her mother tearfully expressing her sadness at being helpless in the face of Tara's impending death. Tara expressed her deep sadness about not being around to see her son grow up. There was also hope in her words – that Luke would have a childhood as happy as she had. In a way, there was a huge sense of relief in the moment, for both of them. It wasn't as awkward or as difficult as her mother thought it might be. There was a beautiful honesty in what they had just shared.

Over the following days, with the support of the hospice team, the rest of Tara's family came to understand this deep and real need for her too. They realised that Tara needed this conversation, and indeed many subsequent conversations, to prepare her for a peaceful letting go to death.

I still remember my final conversation with Tara.

'I often wonder, will Luke even remember me? I like to think that he would,' she admitted. 'But I know George will be a great father, and my mother and sisters will be there for Luke, too. I'd love to have seen him start school. I'd love to have taken him on trips.' Even though Tara had told her story with her family as she'd wanted to, there was still the reality of all of the parts of her story she would be missing out on, which was so desperately sad.

But she had prepared herself for her final letting go as much as she could by having many meaningful conversations with family and friends. She had shared her funeral requests, and the details of her life's story, and in this sharing had created new memories with her loved ones. All of this helped her to find a measure of peace in her final days.

As a child I was most fortunate to grow up in a village that had a great oral tradition of storytelling. From my earliest memory I recall the many stories told within families of a great giant named Droim Dearg who lived in the hills overlooking our village of Ballindooley. It was said that this giant was a member of the ancient Fianna, whose leader was the famous Finn MacCool. The stories always presented him as a kindly giant who, from a distance, watched over our village and our people, someone who would protect us. These stories and the art of storytelling passed down through the generations; I continued to share this particular story about Droim Dearg with my nieces and nephews, and they in turn are now sharing it with their young families.

In their purest form, stories teach us important life lessons – about recognising good and bad, right and wrong, and about the consequences of our actions. In childhood stories, things are often simple – evil is defeated and there is a happy ending – and the stories we hear as children encourage us to open up our imaginations to life's great possibilities. But as we move away from childhood and these types of stories, this view of story soon disappears to be replaced by an adult view which is often more closed-off. As the outer world becomes more demanding (and this is often even the case for children, these days), we stop going to our inner rooms, shutting the door, walking into the wardrobe and entering the world of soul. As we get to adulthood, we stifle the imagination that life's journey requires. The sharing of story, in particular our own story, can clarify our thoughts, and give insight and meaning to our experiences. In a sense to tell our story is to share our own invaluable sense of life.

Life is story. I think we need to be reminded every single day that we are part of a bigger story, part of something greater than ourselves, and that each of our stories matters, a great deal. To be reminded of that truth is to live in hope.

CHAPTER 6

Feelings of Loss and Grief

We experience loss with the heart. It can be deep and painful, and it can heal cleanly or leave a scar. Just as the body works miracles of healing on itself, the heart also naturally knows how to heal from the pain of loss. We can't help but have losses – they are part of a normal life. But we can learn to take care of ourselves so the wound heals cleanly. And I am not only referring to big losses here. As significant as they are, they may not account for the majority of losses that we go through in a lifetime. It's the many little losses we experience day after day, year after year, such as hurt pride or being overlooked at work, that add up. Thousands of small hurts and losses can accumulate in a heart and create a growing wound that makes for a deeply wounded person.

Loss doesn't necessarily only refer to bereavement: you can think of loss as any event that changes the way things have been. In some way, the world you have gotten used to is suddenly different. When people talk about losses they're most often referring to the big losses like a death, the break-up of a family or a long-distance move. But dealing with smaller losses is important too, because knowing how to cope with these will in great measure help us cope with big losses.

Loss is what happens; grief is how people feel as a result. Sometimes grief is powerful and complicated. Other times it is not at all hard to get through, especially if the person you are grieving has enjoyed a long and fruitful life. Often, this grief journey can generate a sense of gratitude, as in 'We're grateful we had her for so long'. But all losses generate feelings. How people handle a loss depends on how they are put together. It depends on what they have learned about handling loss from their cultural background and from their families. It can also depend on what has already happened in their lives, what they have had to deal with. If we avoid expressing our feelings about loss, it means the feelings have to go underground and can affect our lives moving forward.

As well as grief after loss, we may also experience anticipatory grief – something that happens when death is inevitable – where a person or family takes time to be with their feelings and consider taking actions that might not be possible after the loss: things like saying goodbye, sharing stories and memories that give meaning to what we experience, that can enable us to create a world that is both habitable and hospitable.

Olive's Story

Olive was diagnosed with motor neurone disease in her early fifties. Originally from Scotland, she had moved to Ireland in her twenties to work as a nurse and then she met and married Mike, who Olive talked of as being her anchor and strength through her diagnosis. She had six adult children and lived a very active and full life. Working with adults who were visually challenged, she used her voice to become a great advocate for this vulnerable group of people, both locally and nationally. Olive's love of her work was palpable. She found that outside of her love and care for her husband and family, it provided a good balance in her life, and she was proud of the work she did.

At the outset of her diagnosis, Olive had no real concept of what motor neurone disease was, and it was a huge shock to her when she started to read up on how it can progress. This was a time in her life when her children were more or less fending for themselves, and she was looking forward to a different stage of life, one where she could focus on herself and her husband and, in the distance, grandchildren. As growing awareness of the progression of her disease dawned, she worried about how it would impact her and the members of her family.

The nature of motor neurone disease means that not only is there a physical loss of mobility, but a patient also eventually loses their voice. This is something that has been their foremost means of communication for so long, and it can be a very distressing experience for them. Often they have to resort to new and different ways of communication, something that can be very frustrating.

Olive talked openly about how difficult it was for her to process the different and difficult stages of letting go that this disease presented over two years from diagnosis. Her first admission to the hospice was into her second year of diagnosis. Her mobility was declining and she was having difficulty expressing herself verbally.

On one particular day as Olive and I reflected on her life, it was most evident that she was grieving the loss of her own life, her future plans professionally, and most of all, a future with her husband and family. She was especially distraught at the painful knowledge that she might not live to see the birth of her grandchild, which was due in a few months' time.

There were many, many tears of grief through the next couple of days as she became aware of how limited her time was. At this point, she was beginning to lose her voice and was frightened about how having problems communicating her feelings would affect her.

One afternoon a week later, one of our volunteers went into Olive's room to give her a manicure. This is usually a soothing and enjoyable treatment, but in this instance, Olive was visibly uneasy, as it brought home to her the deterioration of her motor skills.

'This is what it has come to,' she sighed, smiling a little. 'I always used to love doing my own nails – the brighter, the better. One more thing I have to let go of, I guess.'

Her grief was indeed very raw and at times overwhelming, anticipating the loss of all that she loved deeply. We explored together if there was any particular piece of work that might in some measure give meaning to her devastating sense of loss.

I knew she was a bright woman, who always had a hardback diary with her – something she used to communicate with us, giving her voice a rest, and to write down her feelings and thoughts.

'What would it be like for you to write your life experiences in a book?' I suggested to her. 'It might give order to them. Perhaps through the medium of writing, you might give solid expression to the idea of letting go.'

Knowing that her arms now had limited mobility, we sourced a voice-to-text app for her to use and Olive began to 'write' the story of her life, via the miracle of dictation. Through this process, she found a new freedom when it came to expressing herself. Feeling a little better in herself, she decided to return home, knowing that her deterioration was progressing and wanting to spend time with her family. Olive found great support from her psychologist and care team who facilitated her many needs around writing her book.

Eventually, Olive had her final admission to hospice for end-of-life care. Although her mobility had gone completely and her voice was near ending, the sense of who she was was still very apparent. All the while, she still wore her trademark slash of bold lipstick. Nearing the end, she relied on her sisters to apply it for her.

By this time, Olive had a completed a first draft of her story, after four months of dedicated support and help from family, community and professionals. With her limited voice, she had written her life story, detailing her own childhood, the births of her children and the great strides she had made professionally. The chapters addressed to her family would be available to them into the future, and in turn, her grandchildren. She was so visibly proud of it all. She was deteriorating daily, but hopeful that she might see her story as a finished book.

Mindful of this deterioration, her support team emailed the text to the hospice, and with the support of our medical secretary, Yvonne, we had the book printed off and bound beautifully in a light pink colour, with Olive's proposed title and, most of all, her name on the cover as the author of this, her book. A few days later, I took it to Olive's bedroom.

'Olive,' I said to her. 'This is your book.'

Fully aware of what lay in front of her, Olive managed a big smile. It had happened. Her finished book was finally here. Later, taking comfortable armchairs, fresh scones and tea into Olive's room, her sisters and friends decided through the afternoon to read the book aloud for Olive. There were many tears and much laughter, but most of all a deep sense that a life lived to the full was being celebrated. Olive had indeed given expression and deep meaning to a wonderful life.

Soon after that gathering, I came into work early one morning to learn that Olive had died a couple of hours earlier. I visited her room, and her husband Mike was there, holding her hand.

Her book, which looked larger than life, had pride of place on her bedside locker.

Olive had travelled to her inner depths to experience her peace and healing; she had in a sense walked through her life. And this really helped her to process all that she was losing and grieving for. The soul really desires to know our own story for healing, and this will bring a sense of wholeness to the dying person. Any practice that will take you from your head to your heart is a journey towards healing.

After Olive's passing, I thought deeply about how fragile our lives can be, and how limited they can become in such a short period of time. There's little we should take for granted in life.

One of the best things to do when you experience a sense of loss or grief is to give yourself permission to cry. It is a very healthy way to express your feelings. Crying helps when we can't find the words we need, or words can't fully convey what we're feeling. In his writings on grief, *A Grief Observed* C. S. Lewis tells us that tears are like the rain. They loosen up our soil so we can grow in different directions. But when we become adults in this life, we are conditioned to feel we need to apologise for our tears, feeling that they are a sign of failure, weakness or negativity. I often welcome tears. They are so integral to the human condition.

Skills for growing through loss and grief are mostly about learning how to take good care of yourself while you naturally go through the process of healing. Taking time out just to be, and feel, and think about what was and will be important are all very special opportunities that can come with a loss experience. Being open to these important moments is a way to honour our loss and to linger in the humanness of the experience.

Moving on is an important part of the grieving process. It means you are accepting your loss, but that's not the same as forgetting. It is possible to move on with your life and still keep the memory of someone or something you lost as an important part of you. If you follow a religious tradition, embrace the comfort its mourning rituals can provide. Spiritual activities that are meaningful to you – such as praying, meditating or going to church – can offer solace. Non-religious mourning rituals may involve the simple lighting of a candle alongside a photograph of your loved one; taking reflective walks in nature, by the sea; a daily journal expressing your feelings. If you are questioning your faith in the wake of your loss this is normal. Perhaps you might like to talk to someone in your faith community. This is a time to be gentle with yourself, to have self-compassion and to acknowledge that you have experienced a significant loss that needs time to heal.

Silvie's Story

When I first met Silvie, it was a bright, sunny spring morning. She was thirty-eight years of age and married to Brian, with four young children. Accompanied by her sister, Silvie chatted to me in a general way about family and home during this first meeting. Her youngest was six, and her eldest was twelve. She had carved out a career in marketing abroad when she was in her twenties, and when her children came along, herself and Brian made a decision to return to Ireland to bring up their young family close to extended family. On returning to Ireland, Silvie made a decision that she would devote herself to becoming a full-time mother.

Through subsequent weeks Silvie and I had many long conversations over a cup of tea or a walk in the hospice garden. She was open and engaging about life and her illness. She talked openly about her shock diagnosis of cancer, its impact on her and her family life. She spoke about the fear of the reality facing her and not being able to contemplate letting go of her much-loved children. Silvie's family had returned to Ireland to buy their first home here, and before her diagnosis, they had been embarking on a future that they had worked hard and planned for. Silvie was creative by nature and availed of art therapy at hospice to give expression to the raw feelings of grief that she was experiencing. She talked of the many plans and hopes they still had as a family, plans she was hoping to achieve in the time she had left.

Silvie had three admissions to the hospice Inpatient Unit over six months, during which time she became ever more adept, with the support of the medical social workers and pastoral care, at facing head-on her deepest questions about life, 'Why? Why now? I wish I had more time with the children – what will the future hold for them? Why do I have to die?' There was so much heartache and so much emotional pain being poured out from the depths of her soul.

Silvie had an awareness of her own mortality which had a significant impact on what she considered essential through her final days. She got to go home for some hours daily to be with her husband and children in their familiar environment. It was during these times together that Silvie had the necessary chats with her young family about a future without her presence, imparting the gentle advice of a mother to guide and prepare her children as best she could for their years ahead.

Our hospice medical social work team, a team specifically trained to work in a hospice environment, was always available to Silvie, Brian and their young children. If required and needed, they would ordinarily talk a parent of young children through how to broach these difficult conversations, and what type of language to use. The social worker would take the lead from the child, and there would often be a variety of play therapies available that would help lead into the conversation. An individual approach is always necessary – children ask very direct questions. Although each child is different, and each child's baseline understanding of illness and death is different, it's so important to have open conversations with them.

Children digest this information differently from adults. One minute, you can be talking about death with them, and the next they might ask, 'Can I read that storybook?' But that doesn't mean that they don't understand, or that they're not grieving. They process these emotions and feelings in their own way, and in their own time.

It was now September, and as the children returned to school, Silvie began to deteriorate. Too unwell for any further visits home and aware that her time was limited, Silvie had one final request. Her youngest boy, Jake, was to have his seventh birthday in five days: they had talked about this very important birthday in the family, and he looked forward to celebrating it. As a hospice team, guided by Silvie, we put a plan in place for her young boy to celebrate his birthday with her, his family and school friends at hospice. Though not a regular occurrence, birthday parties of young children can and do happen here. Some of the hospice team had children of a similar age, so the stark reality of what Silvie was going through certainly faced us all.

Our Day Care Unit is a warm, inviting space and was decorated appropriately for a seventh birthday party by staff nurse Emer. Invitations were sent to Jake's friends. Birthday cake was ordered, along with lots of refreshments and gifts for children, all carefully prepared by hospice staff, with a lingering sadness in the air. At Silvie's request, we invited a magician to entertain the children. Jake had asked her the previous week, and she was determined to fulfil this last request for him.

That mid-September Friday was a most beautiful autumn day, filled with bright sunshine that danced into the room, all ready for Jake's party, through the autumn-coloured trees outside. It was the seventh birthday of a very special boy, and his mother was just two doors away down the corridor, in her hospice bed. Sadly, Silvie had deteriorated significantly overnight and was now unresponsive. I dropped into her room, sat quietly beside her bed and shared with her the details of her boy's birthday, to be celebrated in three hours, assuring her that we were honouring her very important request that her son would have his birthday close to her. There was no response from Silvie, but my hope was that she heard me at some level.

At twelve noon, we opened our doors to the joy and wonder of seven-year-olds. Silvie's children arrived with their dad, supported by our hospice medical social worker, Aisling, who had developed a close and warm bond with the family. Jake asked to visit his mum.

When staff nurse Emer took the family to her room, Jake leaned into the bed to tell his mum it was his birthday. Amazingly, Silvie opened her eyes, extended her arms to hold him and said, 'Happy birthday'. Those were Silvie's final words. School friends, accompanied by their teachers, arrived for the birthday party, as did Jake's granny and grandad. Games were played, magic happened, 'Happy Birthday' was sung, and the children enjoyed themselves, exactly as Silvie would wish. And when the party came to an end at about five o'clock, hospice CEO Mary Nash and I stood silently at the hospice door, mugs of tea in hand, as we watched Jake, holding his gifts and birthday balloons, make his way through the car park with his family to return home. Her final request honoured, Silvie let herself go to death quietly and peacefully at 8 p.m. that evening.

Like Olive, Silvie had been grieving all that she was losing but she prepared herself as best she could for this loss, and indeed the loss those she loved would experience when she was gone, by having open, honest conversations with them, and by spending as many special moments with them as she could.

The soul work that happens through my pastoral care work with patients is quiet, subtle and nearly impossible to put into words. However, what I experience is the transformation into an authentic human being, a person who has grown to embrace their fragility and vulnerability alongside their resilience and inner strength. Their sadness has found a home in the shelter of their inner peace; the light of their soul has come to illuminate their being. They have come home to themselves. The thirteenth-century Persian mystic, Rumi tells us:

There is a life-force within your soul,
seek that life.

There is a gem in the mountain of your body,
seek that mine.
O Traveller, if you are in search of That,
Don't look outside, look inside yourself and
seek That.

CHAPTER 7

The Sacred Art of Dying

How we die is a profoundly personal journey. Each person's death is unique, and there is nothing more crushing for a dying person than to be isolated and abandoned. Telling and listening to stories breaks the sense of isolation. Dying is, unavoidably, an experience of the loss of control. In the process of reviewing one's life in order to let it go, the dying person ties up loose ends so to speak, getting 'their affairs in order'. Adopting this mindset is a constructive and practical alternative to the terror of losing control, and will pave the way for embracing the sacred aspect of dying.

Richard Groves, author of *The American Book of Living and Dying,* suggests that the sacred art of dying can give us an edge in recognising the natural processes of dying. As the body shuts down, more attention is given to inner awareness. What might appear to be a diminished expression of character and personality could indicate a radical shift in priorities, which is not necessarily bad. Death, for all of us, ultimately involves an ending and a yielding, a recognition that our old familiar life is no longer sustainable.

Steve Jobs, co-founder and CEO of Apple Computers, died in 2011 having suffered with cancer for a number of years. As he faced the end of his life, aged fifty-six and worth an estimated ten billion dollars, he is reported to have reflected on his success and wealth and realised that while he could not bring these things with him on this last journey, he would be bringing happy memories and the love he felt for his family and friends. This final realisation of what truly mattered, what should truly be treasured, was a very important part of his death.

Just before he died, Steve is said to have

looked at his sister Patty, then for a long time at his children, then at his wife, Laurene, and then over their shoulders past them. His final words were: 'OH WOW! WOW! OH WOW!' Whatever he saw before he left, we don't know, but it must have been quite wonderful. At this point, Steve had reached a point where he was finally open to accepting the sacred art of his death.

It's not uncommon for patients, in the moments leading up to their death, to have their own vision of the Divine. It's almost as if the other world – the world of eternal life – is beckoning to them. I've been present many times when this has occurred. This moment has always seemed to signal joy and peace. That they are met with a beatific vision often comes as a surprise to them. It's almost like a moment of clarity before death. It's a hugely humbling experience to be in the presence of the dying when they do experience this.

Often, I am asked by friends and others what a ministry of journeying with people towards their death has taught me. And perhaps more than anything, it has taught me more about life and how to engage as best I can with this gift of life, whatever the circumstances. Each death in a way reflects my own coming death and leads me to reflect on the finiteness of our earthly life and what I am making of my life. The time we spend on this Earth is so limited – we must spend it wisely.

Madge's Story

Sometimes an elderly person can have a sense of their imminent death, and they can begin to withdraw naturally from the world around them and into their inner world. Families can worry, even though it can often be a very peaceful process for the patient. Their loved one's final letting go is beginning in a very gentle way.

Madge was a perfect example of this. A lively lady of eighty-five, Madge enjoyed the company of other residents for bingo and card playing in the nursing home in which she lived. However, her family was concerned that Madge seemed withdrawn of late and less interested in daily activities. One day, I went to visit her in the nursing home, on referral from Jane, a hospice community nurse, who felt that Madge might benefit from pastoral care support.

Madge was comfortably wrapped up in her bed, and spoke with a gentle, calm, yet determined voice. We talked through her life story.

'I came from a farming background and lived close with nature, and that really informed how I lived my life,' she smiled. 'Just in harmony with all things farming.'

She looked out over the green pastures beyond the nursing home, with a view of animals grazing seasonally. Very often for a hospice patient, their view of the world becomes very limited, so what they can see from their window becomes even more significant and important than usual.

Speaking of her adult children, she said, 'The kids are great – they come to see me every day, but you know, recently, they've been asking me why I'm not up and seated out of bed more,' she said. 'I'm quite content just to be in bed, if I'm honest. I like to lie here and to think about what lies ahead for me. I know my end is coming, and I'm happy enough about that. I've lived my life.'

She was concerned that this change might be upsetting for her family, knowing that their care for her wellbeing was of great importance. Very often this is the reason behind a family's desire to have their loved one active and up and about. They wanted reassurance that she was doing well and still reasonably mobile. Yet sometimes the true need of the patient is forgotten amid all of this.

We explored her sense of withdrawing. Madge, who appeared to be very self-aware, felt that this was part of her spiritual journey and was happy to begin to change her focus from the external world to her inner one. Madge was a prayerful lady, who had a great sense of where this soul journey was taking her and willing to begin her letting go calmly and quietly with what I felt was a depth of serenity.

Talking to the nursing home's clinical nurse manager after my visit, I said, 'Madge has expressed a wish that she'd like to stay in bed. She'd like to rest peacefully. I know this is a sensitive issue, but it might be nice if you could have this conversation with her family, that Madge is comfortable in her beginning to let go.'

A couple of months after Madge's peaceful death, I received a letter in the post from Madge's family, expressing their gratitude for being able to set aside their own needs and be attentive to the needs of their mother for her final days. They wrote at length of their own diverse needs for their mother, a need to be active and doing things for her, while forgetting to listen to what her needs might be. They wrote in particular of their coming together, a large family, keeping vigil with their mother.

I had not met in person with Madge's family, but as I reflected on their letter, I was grateful that Madge was able to spend her final days as she wished and that her family were there to accompany her through those days. The sacred art of dying is unique to each person; it is a journey they alone can take. But in the company of family and friends, it can be comforting for both.

Jade's Story

Jade was a thirty-year-old professional who had been admitted for end-of-life care, and it was possible her death would happen within days. The first time I saw her, Jade's youth was so striking to me. I could see that her illness had really taken its toll, yet her beautiful essence was still there. Her face was framed by a feminine and modern brunette wig. Her make-up and perfumes took pride of place on her bedside locker, and a huge bouquet of fresh lilies sat in the corner.

Jade and her fiancé Ivan talked of their desire to marry before her untimely death. Though visibly unwell, Jade talked of the dream for her wedding day since her marriage proposal from Ivan three years ago. Her cancer diagnosis had delayed all of their plans. Tears shone in her eyes as she said, 'We've thought of this day for so long. But it's important for us to have it now. I really wish it was another way.'

Could we as a hospice team facilitate this very important need? Through that evening, with the support of the hospice team and close friends, we began to put a plan in place, knowing that time was limited. Two creatively minded friends of mine, Carmel and Connie, agreed to decorate the hospice chapel and provide the liturgical music. We talked with Joe, our hospice chef, about providing a four-course wedding banquet for a small number of guests. Both Jade and Ivan had reflected on their special day and requested a simple, quiet ceremony of a Catholic Mass in the hospice chapel, with family and some close friends. We were to take our guidance from Doctor Ita, our medical director and hospice consultant in palliative medicine, on just how limited Jade's time might be. We were advised to arrange things for her wedding to Ivan sooner rather than later, as sadly Jade's condition was deteriorating daily.

So we decided on Sunday afternoon, just two days away.

We invited a local bridal company to visit the hospice and attend gently and sensitively to Jade's bridal dress requests and those of her sister, who would be her bridesmaid. Jade wanted to get married in a white wedding dress, and she chose one herself, from a wide selection in her hospice bedroom. The atmosphere bubbled with lightness and jubilation, just like it might with any bride and her bridesmaid excitedly getting ready for the big day. For a short while, the illness was completely forgotten and there was laughter as they made decisions on dress details and accessories. Our hospice volunteer hairdresser and make-up artist were also most happy to accommodate.

I sat with Jade for some time on Saturday as she gave detailed thought to her wedding day Mass booklet – like any bride, Jade expressed joy and excitement about her wedding just twenty-four hours away. But she was also clearly struggling with the reality of facing the end of her life, as might happen with anyone of that age in her situation, questioning deeply the 'why' of the moment and the 'why not' of the future. The poignancy of the wedding added another layer to her emotion. Still, she was so grateful for the support of the team and that she and Ivan would become husband and wife, a longed-for dream that they shared since their engagement.

Brightly lit lanterns adorned the corridor leading to the hospice chapel, and chamber music played in the background as we anxiously awaited Jade to emerge in her wheelchair from her hospice bedroom. Under the watchful eye of Doctor Ita, Jade, her parents and sister quietly made their short journey from her bedroom to the chapel. She was the most beautiful bride; determined and smiling broadly.

Ten steps away from the chapel, Jade asked her parents to pause.

'I want to walk in to Ivan,' she said firmly. On each side, her parents held her and they all entered to the strains of 'Ode to Joy'. There, she was met by Ivan who became her husband thirty minutes later.

With a mixture of emotions, Jade and Ivan joined their wedding guests of twenty in the hospice dining room for their elegant wedding banquet. Jade was grateful to have one hour with her family and friends, after which she returned to her bedroom for some much-needed rest.

Our hospice photographer, Joe, worked through the night and arrived early on Monday to present Jade and Ivan with their wedding photographs, which they pored over with family and friends quietly through the day.

My final visit with Jade on Monday evening was deeply emotional for her. She had begun to say goodbye to visiting family and friends for the last time.

'I have a real sense of peace now,' she told me. 'I've lived with a really fantastic intensity, these last few days.' She acknowledged that her heart was broken at the prospect of saying goodbye so soon, but that through this painful brokenness hers had become a heart that had come to know love deeply. Jade died in the arms of Ivan, now her husband, on Tuesday morning.

Death has the power to heal because it has the power to put life into perspective with an awareness of life's important priorities. Therefore, the art of dying can indeed become the art of living.

Mary Oliver has a beautiful poem titled 'When Death Comes'. It paints a vivid picture of a person who has embraced their mortality, and their true self. In the poem, Oliver imagines the end of her life and talks about wanting to be able to say that she lived her life fully, with courage and compassion, and faces death with acceptance.

Very often as I complete a life review with a patient, they may ask, 'Is there anything after death – is there another life?' This question is asked by those who do not identify with any religion as much as those who do.

Several world religions have their own beliefs surrounding what happens after death.

The Catholic teaching is that of the Resurrection. Christ himself went through the door of death, but he returned, having been raised from death by the Father. His message is that of eternal life, as He tells us in John's Gospel that he has gone to prepare rooms for us in His Father's house. In the preface of the Mass for the dead, we hear the words, 'Lord, for your faithful people life has changed, not ended.'

In the traditions of Judaism and Protestantism, it is believed that resurrection will come at the end of time after the last judgement. The Orthodox Church speaks of the afterlife as the heavenly

Jerusalem, which symbolises the Kingdom of God, a state of life in His presence.

For Muslims, the Quran describes paradise as a beautiful garden, where those who are chosen live a perfect life for all eternity, in union with God.

In the Hindu tradition, there is a belief that humans are in a cycle of death and rebirth called 'samsara'. When a person dies, their soul is reborn in a different body.

For Buddhists, the spirit does not die; it reincarnates itself. Buddhists aim to free themselves from the cycle of reincarnation – having to pass from one life to the other – based on good and bad actions. And atheists are often quite willing to consider the idea of an afterlife.

At the end of their lives, people often find themselves urgently asking questions about what may lie beyond, a question which none of us truly knows the answer to.

None of us has the final answer on this, but for myself, at the moment of my death, I hope that Jesus will be there on the other side, to lead me to the House of the Father.

Paula's Story

Paula, a sixty-year-old woman, was married to Harry, with a daughter, Moya, who was in her early twenties. Paula was a pharmacist, and ran her self-owned pharmacy in a busy suburban area of town. She came from a well-respected family of pharmacists and medics, and had a reputation far and wide in Galway as a pharmacist of great insight. Paula already had an intimate knowledge of cancer even before her own cancer diagnosis, as many customers would confide in her about their own symptoms as they filled their medication prescriptions.

She came to the hospice for end-of-life care and was there for just five weeks. In preparation for her death, Paula had reflected on her letting go of her connection to life's material possessions; however, it was the letting go of her close family, Harry and Moya in particular, that caused great spiritual pain for Paula. Her love for both of them was a bond which could not be broken.

'I'm especially worried that Harry will withdraw, and not draw on the support of people around him to carry him through the years ahead,' she admitted. But she hoped that other loved ones would rally around her husband and daughter and help them cope during a difficult time, supporting them in ways Paula wished she could but would not be able to.

Through tears and indeed much laughter, we completed Paula's life review, and moved on to plan and write her funeral liturgy. She was a committed Catholic with great love for sacred scripture, so great attention was given to her funeral scripture readings.

She was quite emphatic in her wishes, stressing, 'I want uplifting passages of scripture that will console those who are listening, especially Harry and Moya.' In the end, she decided on a piece from John's Gospel.

*Do not let your hearts be troubled. Trust in
God still, and trust in me.
There are many rooms in my Father's house.
If there were not, I should have told you. I
am going now to prepare a place for you.
(John 14: 1-2)*

These sacred words would convey love, empathy, and compassion during her funeral Mass. Having completed and written Paula's funeral liturgy, I presented it to her. Quietly and tearfully she glanced through her chosen work, as I left her room to allow time and space for reflection.

My next meeting was with both Paula and Harry. She talked through her thoughts about what the experience of death might be for her. She explored her sense of an afterlife and if she might ever have an awareness of how Harry and Moya were living their lives. People, especially mothers, often ask these questions: 'Will I ever have a sense of them? Will I be able to guide them from the beyond?'

All I can offer is a listening ear. I have to listen with my heart, more than anything. I don't have answers, but I'm not sure Paula was looking for answers. She was trying to make sense of an afterlife for herself. Usually people aren't expecting answers when they ask this question. That knowledge is not available to us in this life, but there's a hope that one is going somewhere without suffering and pain, and that in some way you might have a sense of your loved ones.

'All you can do is wonder, really,' Paula said. 'You'd like to think you might be able to be in people's lives, even in some tiny kind of way.' It was both an emotional conversation and a deeply intimate moment that was, I believe, healing for both of them. Harry, though tearful, was able to share in this important conversation with Paula, by acknowledging that it was difficult for him also to let go of Paula, but that both himself and Moya would never forget the many great years they all had together. I believe it really helped her on this journey of letting go of her loved ones and feeling more assured that they would be okay after she was gone.

Paula found great comfort and spiritual strength in the company of her cousin and close friend Father Michael, who visited her almost daily. Paula had looked at the totality of her life events and availed well of the opportunity to see her life in context, as a whole. She was now able to rest peacefully, having prepared herself emotionally and spiritually for the sacred art of dying. Her inner work was now complete as she awaited the final letting go to death.

All of the letting go that we do throughout our life – letting go of anger, resentment, emotional pain, of worldly possessions through the making of your will, and the emotional letting go of family – all of this makes the passage of letting go to death much easier.

John's Story

John came from my home parish of Castlegar; something that immediately bonded us. He was a family man, who had enjoyed the outdoors for years. Even now, I smile at memories of his quirky and dry sense of humour, which always took me by surprise. He worked as a greenskeeper at the award-winning five-star hotel Glenlo Abbey. Each week he would share the stories of his family – wife Ann, son Dermot and two grandchildren. He talked of his other son, Paul, who had died tragically some years earlier in a car accident. John found it difficult to talk about Paul, but each week, little by little, he shared details of Paul's life, and finally he was able to share his own painful experience as a parent on hearing the news of the tragic death of his son.

'He was coming from Belgium, where he lived, and travelling home from Dublin to be with us early in the new year,' John recalled. 'We had planned a game of golf together the following day. Instead of enjoying the time together as a family, we had to go through the agony of organising his funeral.'

John was very honest and each week he was able to share how he was deteriorating – more pain one week, slower mobility the next – until finally he needed an admission to hospice as an inpatient for end-of-life care.

In his last days, he talked openly and honestly about what death meant for him.

'I have no fear of death, because I have a sense I will meet with Paul again. That gives me great comfort,' he said.

Early one morning as I sat with John, Dermot was seated alongside his father. He was a tall, strong Garda sergeant, who was at ease in his vulnerability, as he kept vigil with his father.

'When I was passing by one of the rooms, I saw through the door there was a lovely little altar set up with a crucifix and a light,' he told me. 'Could we have one of those for my dad, do you think?'

'Let's go and ask your dad if he might like one,' I replied. John was delighted with the idea.

There was a beautiful tone to Dermot's voice as he made this request; a gentleness from a son who wished his father to have every spiritual comfort as he approached death. I reflected afterwards on the quiet strength of this young man who had taken endless time to be with his father.

As I touched on earlier in the chapter, ritual is important through the dying process. It can address our need to understand our existence in a more meaningful way. It can provide a pathway, as we move from one stage of life to the next. Ritual occurs within sacred time and space, and it needs to be marked, simply by the lighting of a candle or through the Sacrament of Anointing. In doing so, the sacred ritual is powerful. For a family, ritual can indicate the coming towards the end. It can, in its own quiet way, provide a great comfort. Within the mystery of death, you can feel accompanied in many ways by the Divine.

CHAPTER 8

Loneliness

Is there anyone who has never felt the pain of loneliness, who has never known the lonely pain of isolation and separation? Is there anyone who has never suffered the lonely pain of rejection or the loss of love when disconnected from a partner in a relationship?

When loneliness feels all-consuming, it can be harmful to our health and wellbeing. But there are degrees of loneliness and what one person experiences as lonely, another may not. For that reason, being specific about what exactly makes you feel isolated and lonely can be beneficial. Perhaps it could be a geographic move away from family and friends; a relationship break-up; having no close friends – just acquaintances and colleagues; being at a different life stage to those around you. Sometimes when you identify exactly why you feel lonely, you may be able to take steps to address it.

There is a world of difference between loneliness and aloneness. Aloneness occurs when we are on our own and are able to accept ourselves as we are. There is a feeling of contentment that we and the people in the world around us are okay. Loneliness, on the other hand, can be the most crushing feeling that any of us can experience. Loneliness is sometimes about being on our own and at other times about *feeling* we are on our own; perhaps we are finding it difficult to accept ourselves or fit in and feel abandoned by others. Whether we feel lonely or alone will be determined by the relationship we have with ourselves, and by our relationships with others.

People may be familiar with the idea of loneliness, but the term 'spiritual loneliness' is unfamiliar to many. Still, it's a very real type of loneliness. In a world that is increasingly secular, spiritual loneliness has become much more prevalent, if less talked about.

This loneliness of the spirit is not a longing for a specific person or the urge to have contact with others. It is a sense of inner emptiness, which cannot be overcome by being with others. It is a sense of incompleteness. Spiritual loneliness is a void we feel within ourselves. It's a sense of being unfulfilled and lacking wholeness.

Interpersonal loneliness affects just part of our lives but spiritual loneliness affects every dimension of our lives; it is felt at a deep level within us.

So how do we fill this inner emptiness called spiritual loneliness? This inner void can be filled through many means, but mainly through the grace which is given by God to all persons. Again, so few people understand the concept of grace, but like the air that we breathe, it is something that we cannot see but is there as a gift that we can receive from God. Grace is a divine influence – it gives us spiritual strength to endure the many trials and challenges we experience throughout our lives. Grace nourishes our spirit. Think about how exercise strengthens the physical body: so too does grace strengthen the spiritual self. All we need to do is open ourselves to it.

The principal means of attaining grace come from the sacraments of the Christian faiths, in particular the Eucharist in the Catholic Church, prayer, meditation and charitable or good works. Sacramentals – blessed religious objects, rosary beads, crucifixes, religious pictures, holy medals – are also a means of experiencing grace. We receive sanctifying grace from our daily contact with God – Mass, prayer, scripture reading or simply a chat with Him.

Other faith traditions also have a strong belief in grace. Those who follow the Hindu tradition talk of it as a disposition of kindness and compassion. Buddhists believe that it is the power of good karma – a good action will come back to you as you have given to others – built up over time.

Often a patient might talk about their sense of loneliness caused by being disconnected from God, saying, 'I feel empty inside, I cannot pray anymore. I have lost my sense of God.'

Many of them can feel abandoned by God. Others feel that they don't have the strength or energy to pray, and that they have lost a connection they might have had before. But that connection has never really been lost, and can easily be rebuilt. Even a simple prayer like 'Help me today, God' can be much more powerful than a litany of prayers in restoring that simple conversation with God.

Pauline's Story

Married to Padraig, fifty-year-old Pauline, originally from London, oozed personality. I'd rarely seen her without a smile on her face. She was a true character, with an irrepressible spirit that matched her East End accent.

She and Padraig had their children in their teens and twenties. Each time she came to hospice, usually for symptom control, she toted a brightly coloured bag: 'This is the "me bag",' she would say proudly, taking out her collection of country music and Agatha Christie books.

'Reading takes my mind to a place away from being sick,' she'd say, without a trace of self-pity or sorrow. Her family lived, and her children attended school and college, a lengthy drive away from the hospice, so their visits were late evening and mostly at weekends. Pauline was grateful for the spaciousness and privacy of a large single room, but on occasion I found her tearful and missing her family and the buzz of ordinary life at home.

It was while studying to be a teacher in the UK that she had met Padraig. He had emigrated from Ireland to work as a plumber. Their children were born in the UK, and when Padraig inherited the family farm after the death of his father, they returned to Ireland.

'You should have seen me work a tractor – I would take off like a rocket down the field,' she recalled, laughing giddily. 'I'd just about hear Padraig shouting at me to slow down and take it easy. But the wind was in my hair, and I was so proud of myself, this city girl driving this big tractor through the field.'

While I was having lunch with Pauline in the hospice dining room one day, I noticed that she was not her usual effervescent self.

'I'm so fed up these days. I'm tired of feeling unwell,' she blurted out. 'My world these days is just about medical appointments, taking medication, ringing the bell in my room for assistance for just about everything. I feel so helpless.'

Silence descended for a time. 'Is there anything I can do to help?' I asked.

She turned her face towards me, a request starting to play on her lips.

'Do you know what I would really like?' she said. 'For a few hours I would like to do something just normal. The sun is shining outside. Do you think there's any chance we could just drive to the sea and have an ice-cream?' Such a simple request, yet such an important one.

We agreed to explore the idea with Nicola, who was her nurse for the day. We got the go-ahead – like two girls allowed out from lessons in boarding school – and made a plan to head to the beach in the late afternoon when Pauline felt rested and the sun wouldn't be too strong.

We rescued a wide-brimmed hat from our 'bits and bobs' storage press, and Pauline dressed in a vivid orange linen ensemble. She looked every bit the part of a glamorous day-tripper as we headed for the freedom of the sea and sand. En route, we picked up some ice-creams from the local shop.

'I feel like Shirley Valentine,' Pauline said with laughter in her voice. When we arrived at Ballyloughane, we sat on a bench overlooking the busy beach with the wild Atlantic ocean ebbing and flowing endlessly ahead.

'It's good to see the bigger picture, isn't it?' she sighed. We sat in silence, enjoying the cool ice-cream, listening to the many noises and voices that echoed the contentment and freedom of a day by the sea.

We watched a parent helping his toddler child to walk on the sand.

'I used to walk a lot,' Pauline said. 'I have done a couple of pilgrimage walks, both in Spain and the UK.' Pilgrimage walks, such as the Camino de Santiago, or Way of Saint James, are walks taken on an ancient spiritual path. For people who undertake such a walk, it's often a search for something that's larger and bigger than them.

'I have lost all sense of God,' she continued. 'I have been so angry at what's going on with me, I have not said a prayer for a very long time.'

Then Pauline talked of her interest in visiting old monasteries in the UK, where she felt she always had a sense of the Divine.

'I was always so intrigued by old monasteries and ancient monks,' she revealed. 'I'm lonely for those days, when I felt there was something or someone watching over us – it was comforting.

I wonder if there are any monasteries around here?' she continued. 'I wouldn't mind visiting one some time.'

There was a freedom in being seated overlooking the sea – a place that's immediately evocative for so many people – that allowed Pauline, for a short time, to forget she was a patient in a hospice. Words tumbled out as she talked with laughter of times when she had little materially but was happily in love with Padraig. She talked of a weekly treat both of them enjoyed each Friday evening when they lived in the UK.

'We looked forward to going to the local chipper for good old-fashioned English fish and chips with lots of vinegar,' she said. 'We often shared these stories with the children, and we talked one day of how we would return to the UK for a holiday and together we would all have fish and chips.' She bit down on her lip. 'I guess that day will never come now.'

As we made our way back to the hospice, Pauline asked that we stop at the shop again: she wanted to purchase ice-creams for the nurses.

'Come on,' she commanded. 'We'll take them a treat from the seaside!' And it was a lovely treat, as the nurses were just finishing their day shift to return home. Pauline called out from the doorway of her room, 'Kevin, an ice-cream for you. Nicola, have a cold ice-cream on your way home. Who else is there?' For a few short hours she got to feel like her old self.

A few days later, I contacted a local monastery, that of the Poor Clare sisters. I was aware that they are an enclosed religious order, but hearing the request, they were very happy to have Pauline visit them. So off we went on another adventure, this time through Galway City, where Pauline met with Sister Anthony at the Poor Clare monastery. Sister Anthony is bright and breezy, and very uplifting by nature, and whatever she did for Pauline, it was just the spiritual injection that Pauline needed. She emerged from the monastery with a huge smile. It was a visit that brought great joy and a sense of contentment to her. The sisters extended a further invitation for her to visit, which Pauline was very happy to accept some weeks later. After those visits, she talked of her sense of the spiritual being renewed and feeling her long-lost connection with the Divine beginning to return.

Mindful of the nostalgia around her days of enjoying fish and chips, I contacted a very famous

Galway family fish restaurant, McDonagh's, who were indeed very happy to sponsor this family occasion. I knew that Pauline was deteriorating and would not have the energy required for a family evening out. So with the support of our hospice staff and the restaurant, on a sunny Sunday evening, we organised a restaurant experience for Pauline and her family that took place in her room. Simon, our healthcare assistant, set up a table, dressed with a white tablecloth, silver service and gleaming glassware.

When I went to McDonagh's to collect the food, the woman behind the counter said maternally, 'I added some nice malt vinegar and Fanta orange. Go quick now, so the food will not be cold.' With all traffic lights green, it took but ten minutes to arrive with the food at the hospice on a sun-dappled evening.

Pauline, Padraig and their children had their longed-for fish and chips experience. It may not have been as they wished, but together they shared not just food and the many stories that were told: they shared a togetherness that Pauline often talked fondly about afterwards. It was an occasion that really helped to heal the sense of loneliness she had been experiencing, due to the distance of two hours her family had to travel to be with her.

Listening to Pauline talk about her loneliness, in particular her sense of spiritual loneliness and her longing for what she called her lost connection with the Divine, prompted me to reflect on the importance of spiritual nourishment. We need to be nourished in body, mind and spirit. In ancient traditions, they talked of the 'Five Graces' – sight, sound, touch, smell and taste – all to be honoured in the full experience of life.

To prevent spiritual loneliness, we could reflect on the following:

1. Slow down – listen without trying to compose your next thought. Pause between daily tasks. Take time to be with God, even if you have little time.

2. Spend time in solitude – it may seem counterintuitive, but the antidote for loneliness can sometimes be found in solitude. Spend time outdoors and let nature heal your spirit. Invite God to fill your spiritual tank.

3. Seek the company of others – although some time alone, as mentioned above, is important in order for us to reflect on our thoughts and feelings, connection with others is also very nourishing. We can share our experiences with them, feel part of a larger community, and have fun with them too.

Many people find spiritual nourishment in the shared hopes of a crowd, whether at a religious gathering or at a football match. Some people call these experiences spiritual; some do not. It is not so much the event or the place in itself that is spiritual, but the meaning the person attributes to it. It is not just the music of music festivals. It is the ritual of the camping and the mud and the crowds, all of which together can provide a spiritual euphoria.

Loneliness is inevitable at times. Rather than avoid it by getting busy, look at the reasons for your loneliness. This can be a time of personal growth and can move loneliness towards comfortable solitude, where there can be a deep sense of satisfaction with life.

Enda's Story

Seventy-two-year-old Enda suffered with Parkinson's disease, before he had received his cancer diagnosis. He had been resident in a care home for the past five years and his reason for requesting to meet with a hospice chaplain – which patients in a care home when receiving community hospice care can request – was to ask about how to prepare for death. Enda had a deeply lined face, with strong brown eyes, and had a kindly look about him. Even when dressed in his pyjamas and dressing gown, he wore a peaked tweed cap on his head.

Enda was warm in his welcome when I got to the care home.

'Thanks for coming to see me,' he said with an outstretched hand. After exchanging pleasantries about my journey and the weather, he said softly, 'I often heard from the old people in the village I grew up in that it was good to pray for a happy death.' He wanted to prepare himself spiritually for what lay ahead. He felt a disconnection from the Catholic religion of his childhood, which he had drifted away from through addiction and his sense of not being accepted within the Church as a gay man.

He talked of his many years of challenges with Parkinson's, and his gratitude of being cared for by the professionals in the care home.

'I lived a lonely life for many years,' he said with convincing honesty. 'It was all my own fault. I took to the drink when I was young, and it nearly ruined me.' Enda talked at length about realising in his mid-twenties that he was a gay man.

I suspected he'd had conversations about his sexuality with others, as this revelation came out very naturally; it seemed that he was keen to share this part of himself. I delighted in hearing that he felt comfortable enough with me to talk openly about his sexuality. Still, there was a sense that it was also a struggle central to his life story and had a bearing on the way he'd lived.

Enda talked of feeling very confused about his sexuality for years. 'In my time it was considered a sin,' he explained. 'You just had to hide it.' It was his resulting feelings of confusion and anger that led him to develop an addiction to alcohol.

'I had a good and caring family, but I could not tell anyone in those days. My only way of dealing with it was to get drunk and try to forget,' he continued. 'I was not violent, but I made life hell for everyone. The coming home drunk, the tears my mother cried, the fights with friends.'

Enda talked of the many years of isolating himself from others, feeling he was not worthy of respect because of his addiction. He talked of his deep loneliness in his younger years, and his disconnection from other people and life in general.

In his early fifties, living in Dublin between hostels and on the streets, he was regularly visited by a group of young adults who took food nightly to homeless people. One young lady befriended him and helped him access residential support for his addiction. It was there he came into contact with Alcoholics Anonymous.

'It was the best thing that ever happened to me,' he said. He talked of being under-nourished and in poor health. 'But most of all I realised I was spiritually bankrupt.' He shared that it was through his weekly meetings with Alcoholics Anonymous that he came to the realisation that he needed spiritual support to help him recover from his addiction. He talked of the Twelve-Step programme that he had practised daily for many years as a spiritual programme. He talked in particular of one of the steps that recommends the 'making of a decision to turn our will and our lives over to the care of God as we understand him'.

He found his own relationship with God through a community of like-minded people in Alcoholics Anonymous. After many years of loneliness, this group of people nourished him spiritually and led him to accepting himself for who he was. It was through these meetings that he had finally felt comfortable enough to face what had been troubling him throughout his life.

'It was through the grace of God I found them,' he said, with real gratitude in his voice.

Enda had repaired many broken relationships he'd had through the years. He made contact with family and friends, seeking to rebuild bridges with those he had isolated himself from. He was encouraged through these meetings to accept his sexuality, too.

Enda told me of the moment when he had a conversation with his older sister about his confusing feelings around his sexual identity.

'She couldn't have been more open and receptive and warm about it,' he recalled. 'She said to me, "But you're Enda. You're my brother.

I love you and I've missed you in my life." She then invited me to come west to live close to her.'

Enda had been baptised into the Catholic Church, and had received all the sacraments. However, he had not been to Mass for almost forty years. He now wondered how he could prepare himself to return to the Catholic Church before his death.

He asked if we could have a short time of prayer together. 'I have a longing to hear the old prayers I learned in my youth,' he said shyly. And so we prayed together that afternoon.

Enda met with a local Catholic priest some weeks later, continuing to meet with him until his death, and was happy to return to Mass in the chapel of the care home. He had found himself in a place where he knew what he needed in order to help him have a 'happy death'. Because he had been able to talk about what was going on within himself, his sense of loneliness started to abate. When we are able to name our inner sense of isolation and loneliness, we are on our way towards healing.

It wasn't until Enda got to share his experiences in AA and with his sister that he felt almost whole again. Ultimately, it was through the non-judgemental care of his sister that he found that piece that was missing from within. And then in the final period of his life, he reconnected with the Church and its rituals. Connecting with community and like-minded people gives us a greater sense of who we are. That inner longing that we felt has been bridged. With it, we are free to live our life as it should be lived.

CHAPTER 9

Fear

Possibly the greatest uncertainty in human life is how and when we will die. Very often people fear what they don't understand, and this is very true of death. It is necessary to speak of death as the normal ending to a human life, especially when children ask questions about death – to allow the conversation to be light and just natural, using everyday language. To be honest, I believe the subject of death should be added to the curriculum in schools as part of preparing young people to face life in the years ahead. Normalising and demystifying death – can you think of a more invaluable life lesson? After all, death is not the opposite of life, but the opposite of birth. Fear is a natural emotion and a survival mechanism, and can involve both physical and emotional symptoms. Lots of things make us feel afraid, but, for example, being afraid of fire can keep us safe. Fearing failure can make us try to do well, so that we don't fail, but it can also stop us doing well if the feeling is too strong.

Angie's Story

Angie was seated on the edge of her chair clutching her handbag when we first met. She had received a cancer diagnosis two years earlier, with a short prognosis of one year. A patient can sometimes ask a medical professional, 'How long do I have?' Sometimes, they are told it can be short months or long years. This is not unusual. It's an imprecise science, as is often the case when you're dealing with human life.

However, Angie had survived her prognosis date by almost a year. Living through a time that she did not expect to be alive, Angie had become fearful, with an almost morbid sense that death was constantly around the corner. I don't know that she knew how to accept that. Angie felt that a stay in hospice was signalling the end of her life, and she was not ready to face that fear yet. However, the reason for her proposed admission was for symptom control and to support her around her fear and anxiety. We decided on tentative small steps, the first one being inviting her to the hospice for a short visit.

'This is crazy,' she exhaled. 'I'm sitting here in a hospice, and less than two years ago I was out and about, full of life and energy, running around preparing gardens for horticultural shows. I was at the top of my game. I have lived almost a year longer than what I was given. I know I should be grateful, but the truth is, I wake up every day thinking I might die today.'

The look on her face told me that she was living in what we in hospice would describe as a liminal space; an in-between time. Caught in the headlights, fear can come and live in you. From when we are babies, we crave certainty in almost everything that we do, and this comes from routine and security. To be thrust into a time of uncertainty can be very painful emotionally, even in an instance where a person has outlived a terminal prognosis.

Angie looked much younger than her sixty-one years, with short, blonde curly hair and a face that was flushed pink.

'It's a strange thing to say, but I'm afraid of living and I'm afraid of dying,' she reflected. She pulled her sweater tighter around her and stared into the distance.

'I'm afraid if I move into the hospice I will die here. Does everyone who comes into the hospice die?' she asked.

'Angie, patients come into the hospice for many reasons,' I explained to her. 'Some come for symptom control, to get on top of their pain, some come for a short time of respite, others come one day each week as day care patients. And, yes, patients come to us for end-of-life care too.'

'I have this image of the hospice in my mind,' she admitted. 'It sends a shiver through me.'

'Hospice is brimming with life, Angie,' I replied. 'Before I came to work in hospice myself, I had little idea of what to expect, and I'm not sure I was ready to find out. Yet our patients enjoy art therapy, aromatherapy, a jacuzzi if they wish, and lots more, alongside their medical and nursing needs. There's a lot of activity and life here.'

Angie began to relax a little and sat back in her chair. 'It's a big step to come into the hospice as a patient,' she said. 'It seems very final.' Angie took a long look around her. 'I never thought my life would end like this. In a way, I wish I had gone within the year I was given – this is not living, it's just waiting.'

At the end of the afternoon, Angie agreed to come in the following week for two hours as a day care patient. During that second visit, she sat close to the exit door, giving her a clear path to the outside. Through subsequent weeks as she relaxed a little, she began to chat with other patients and occasionally stayed for lunch.

'I always thought of a hospice as dark and sad, with everyone in bed dying,' she told me then. 'But sitting here, it's bright, and the view of the garden is lovely. I now look forward to my day here each week. This sounds strange, but I had the best laugh of my life here last week when the hairdresser, Mary T, put a purple streak in my hair. I just wanted to go mad and do something different.'

Without her even realising it, life was beginning to bubble up back inside of Angie a little. She wasn't aware of it at the time, but it gave her a measure of courage for what lay ahead.

Angie accepted an admission to the hospice as an inpatient some weeks later. She was now beginning to slowly deteriorate, having less energy and mobility. Though less fearful than she had been, she did at times experience some fear and anxiety. We explored together what this fear felt like for Angie. 'Fear just takes hold of me. I'm frightened of the fear itself,' she said. 'I almost had a panic attack last night, just thinking about that fear.' Angie became tearful at times. 'Sometimes during the night when it's dark and all is quiet, fear just creeps up on me. I know I'm not going to live, I know I'm going to die, but I'm in that in-between place, and it can be very scary.' She wasn't necessarily afraid of the moment of dying; it was just a fear without any specific anchor.

We explored the use of music therapy for relaxation. We chose a comfortable couch in the adjoining conservatory where Angie could stretch out and allow the soothing music and words of relaxation to wash over her and bring rest and calm to her spirit. Angie enjoyed this therapy practice daily, in particular the music of Pachelbel's 'Canon' and 'Serenade'. She put the relaxation apps on her phone, and when fear would take hold, she would listen to the music and let it take her away from her own thinking, to a time and place where she had enjoyed life.

Although Angie had found it difficult to tell her family and friends that she was being admitted into hospice – the finality of that conversation was daunting for her – they were a huge support to her.

Her family and friends arranged for afternoon tea in the hospice garden one sunny afternoon. It was heartening to hear the laughter and the sense of togetherness of the group. 'It was just a wonderful afternoon – they brought in lots of old photographs, and the sharing of stories was great, we laughed so much,' Angie said afterwards. 'They're just a great bunch of people. I felt so free with them. What a pity it took until almost my last days to appreciate their friendship and goodness.'

Angie remained with us at the hospice for four weeks, and talked many times of her unfounded fear of coming in. She often talked of her garden at home that she had landscaped. She was particularly proud of her success at growing many varieties of fruit trees. She missed her garden greatly and decided to return home, where she felt more deeply herself, for the end of her life.

As was the case with Angie, fear makes most of us insecure and vulnerable. Sometimes fear can signal threat but sometimes avoiding something we perceive as a threat can prevent us from involvement in the many challenges and opportunities that lead to growth and learning. Being able to articulate the fear we experience can in good measure increase our ability to face it. Fear can dissolve when we confront the situation we fear head-on.

Like all emotions, fear has a positive side also: it can be a motivator. It was the fear of illness, after all, that led to great advances in medicine. It was the fear of the dark that led to the invention of electricity.

I feel at times the people I meet in hospice, who are trying to cope with the reality of illness and poor health, hold a mirror up to me that reflects my own fears and anxieties. Fear, whether it's of something small or big, has been a constant companion in my life. I have tried to face my fears, though maybe not always successfully. But I'm always tentatively willing to step out of my comfort zone and face fear in the hope that this will result in personal growth. In the past I've had a fear of public speaking; however, my role as chaplain requires a lot of work in that area. I now lead regular prayer services and present education both at hospice and NUI Galway. Stepping out of my comfort zone and learning to work through my fear slowly, I feel much more at ease now in my public presentations.

Mamie's Story

'Why did the priest come to our house?'

I was fourteen, and I had just come over the brow of the hill heading home from choir practice in our local church. I saw in the distance the local priest driving away from our house; not an everyday occurrence by any stretch. There had to be something wrong. Even now, I remember that feeling of foreboding.

'Why was the priest here?' I asked my mother again. She was sitting alone in the kitchen, just staring into the distance. I was aware that my father had gone to London to be with my sister Mamie. She had given birth to a baby two weeks before, which was great news. But I had also overheard hushed talk of her being sick, quiet whispers of the words 'brain tumour'. Despite this, my mother's answer made no sense to me. It could not be true.

'Mamie is dead,' my mother replied quietly.

I had no idea what that meant at that moment. There were no tears. Just silence. The shock had numbed my mother. She had a young family trying to make sense of this shocking news, as she herself was. It was like it was happening outside of us. It didn't take root in my world. I wanted to go away and be on my own, to make sense of it in some way.

Our home was very quiet that evening. Farm work had to be attended to. Supper was late, with little eaten. I wished my father was at home.

Awake in bed through that long night, I tried to remember Mamie's face. I was desperately worried I would forget it, and I searched the darkness for her. I needed to hear her voice; this woman, the eldest of my nine siblings, who was like a second mother to me.

I could hear her many chats with me. One in particular, from about two years before, stood out in my memory: 'Next year you're off to secondary school; try and do your lessons well.' Making your way in life and being your own person was very important to her, even at twenty-five. And she wanted to make sure I had a good future.

Mamie was beautiful, bright and very popular. She looked a lot like my father, with her dark curls and strong blue eyes.

She was full of life – the energy lifted wherever she went. She was always out and about on her bicycle, loved to go to dances, and wore what I thought were the most colourful and beautiful dresses. And she was very caring. She kept an eye on my scoliosis, always reassuring me that one day I would not have to wear a brace, which I felt gave me a special bond with her.

'Make sure you keep wearing the brace,' she told me gently. 'It will keep your spine straight as you grow.'

Registering my despair at having to wear the leather and steel contraption, she put a gentle hand on my shoulder.

'You won't always have to wear it,' she assured me. I longed for the day I could finally return it to the hospital.

She went to London at the age of nineteen to train as a nurse, and it was there that she met

Frank. Within a year, they were engaged and returned home to Galway to be married in our local church.

I remember being up with the dawn on their wedding day. It was a warm, sunny day filled with excitement and frenzy in our family home as we prepared for a very special day.

The image of Mamie as a bride has always stayed with me. It was the very first time I'd seen a bride, and she was beautifully radiant in white satin; almost celestial. Frank was very much the handsome groom. Our youngest sister, Berney, danced about the place, delighted to show everyone her delicate pink chiffon dress. She was seven and as flower girl looked every inch a princess. It was a very happy day. Outside of the church of St Columba's, after the wedding ceremony, we met with extended family, cousins and friends. It was particularly exciting to meet Frank's relatives and friends who had travelled from his home town in West Cork. In the warmth of the summer sun, there was celebration, laughter and great joy.

I was mesmerised by the beauty of the day. The colourful fashion, the glamorous scents, the elegance of brightly lit candles and fresh flowers.

It was just perfect. I felt especially free that day. 'You don't have to wear your brace for this one day,' Mamie had told me. It all felt so special.

Just over a year later, in a state of shock and disbelief, we all returned to St Columba's church. There was no colourful fashion or great joy this time around, for we were here for Mamie's funeral Mass. The stillness and silence among everyone felt strange, heads bowed in mourning for the death of a twenty-six-year-old, who had been a mother for just two short weeks. Listening to my older sisters and the many visitors to our home after the funeral Mass, I tried to piece together words which would help me make sense of the fact that Mamie was dead.

She had been diagnosed with a cancerous brain tumour very early in her pregnancy. Mamie had been aware of the seriousness of this condition. Around five months into her pregnancy she had become critically unwell and her baby daughter Sarah had to be delivered before being transferred to another hospital for neonatal care. She had weighed less than two pounds. Two weeks after Sarah was born, when Mamie was a little stronger, she underwent surgery. My father had been made aware of how critically ill Mamie was and planned to travel to London with my sisters Ann and Margaret to be with her and Frank and their little baby daughter. They were about to take a flight from Dublin, when my father telephoned Frank. They were not prepared for what they heard at the other end of the phone. 'She's gone,' Frank said.

My father, who had always been so close to his first little girl, travelled with Ann and Margaret straight from the airport in London to the hospital mortuary to view Mamie's body. My father remained with Frank, while my sisters returned home to be with us as a family. A few days later, my father and Frank made the long and lonely journey home, both passengers on an Aer Lingus flight that held Mamie's coffin. They had no choice but to leave baby Sarah behind in the hospital, where she was being cared for in the neonatal unit.

Many years afterwards Frank shared that, as he took his seat on this flight, an American tourist seated beside him made small talk about how excited he was to finally be visiting Ireland. Frank explained to him that he was taking the body of his young wife home to Galway for burial. On hearing the story, the gentleman remained reflective throughout the flight. When they were leaving the aircraft, the American tourist gave Frank a silver dollar coin to be given to Sarah as a keepsake, which she holds to this day. Now married with four children of her own, Sarah has her mother's blue eyes, and I like to think she sees the world, in some way, through Mamie's eyes too. Mamie got to see her daughter just once, but never got to hold her. Afterwards, we heard that Mamie held that gaze at Sarah for a long time.

I think of my beloved sister often, remembering the happy times we shared and how much kindness she showed me. But I have also never forgotten the image of Mamie's coffin being received into the church on a sunny July day. I had never seen a coffin before and had never attended a funeral. I kept watching out for her. Her name kept being mentioned by everyone so where was she? Somehow, I expected her to walk around the corner towards us. It was so difficult for me to try to understand that the wooden box in the church held my sister. Because she had travelled from the UK, her coffin was not allowed to be open. I had not seen Mamie dead, and so it took a very long time to come to terms with the idea that I would not see her again. It was so difficult for me to understand that only thirteen months earlier, she had emerged from this same church blissfully happy, with her new husband, looking forward to a future that held endless possibilities. And now Frank was standing at the graveside, exhausted and heartbroken, as they lowered Mamie's coffin into the ground.

For a long time after, I felt all colour had gone from the world. The inconsolable sadness we felt had no words; there was just silence. How could such a beautiful, energetic, young person, who had the promise of a bright and happy future, not be among us anymore?

Revisiting my experience of the death of Mamie has been emotional over the years, but has also given me the opportunity to share this experience with my family. In so doing, it has been a release of emotional pain, and has brought an inner freedom.

The fear I felt when I saw the priest outside my house that day was well founded – the worst thing I could imagine had indeed happened – and it was a very tough experience. Because I had not seen Mamie's deceased body, the grief I felt afterwards was complicated. I kept expecting to receive a letter in the post from her, or half expecting she would come home someday. I feel my fear of death and indeed illness took hold of me at this time.

It's only now, many years later, that I have a deep realisation that no matter how painful the experience of Mamie's death was – and those memories still are – it gave me a great gift. It has nurtured in me a great empathy with the patients and families I have worked with as a chaplain. For that, I'm grateful.

I have discovered over time the emotional value and benefits of talking through my own fears with others and have come to realise that every person has and will experience fear of some kind. Empathy with another person, in particular with the vulnerable, is the ability to sense other people's emotions, and life experience teaches you that. Empathy is at its most powerful when you're in that awful, fearsome place with them. That's when real healing happens.

CHAPTER 10

The Richness of Our Family Tree

Writing this book has taken me down 'Bóithrín na Smaointe' – the byroads of thought. It has also presented an invaluable opportunity to reflect on my own story, reminding me that, like all of us, I am who I am because of those who have been with me and gone before me. The people in our lives, past and present, shape our lives, and often learning of their past experiences helps us to view our own lives through a new lens. The more we can be in touch with the story of our family of origin, the more we can grow in awareness and self-knowledge.

So much is passed on through the generations from our family tree that we have little knowledge of. Looking through old family photographs, we are often surprised to see similarities of appearance: high cheekbones, big ears, striking eyes, a particular smile and many other features. Character traits and temperaments are also passed down, as are behavioural characteristics. Our family tree can be a treasure trove of gifts and talents inherited through the generations – a musical ear, storytelling, a trade or a skill. Attitudes to child rearing, socialising and employment can also be passed on through family. And how we respond to certain events, especially painful ones like bereavement, loss or a sense of injustice, can reflect an enduring family pattern that has been in place for generations.

Many families hold pain that has not been fully processed and so it can be passed on. It could relate to the containing or holding of particular family secrets, a major trauma that was never addressed or land disputes that caused family division, resentment and hatred through the subsequent generations. If a family refuses to process emotional issues, this trait may result in the next generation being unable or ill-equipped to deal with life issues. Perhaps they will avoid and bury painful emotions, or even become unable to engage in meaningful conversation or connection with others.

If you're brought up thinking a certain way, that may end up also being your view of the world. But this can be changed. When we grow up, we may develop the ability to look at a broader world view. It's a choice we have to make.

Sometimes it's only when we experience challenges that this world view opens to us, and we realise that there are ways of thinking that have little to do with the way our family thought.

When we explore the life story of a patient, as in a life review, this piece of work takes both of us into a place of remembering together. The word 'remember' can be broken down to read 're-member': reinstating the memory of a family member back into the family. And as we reflect on a patient's family tree back through the generations we might see that perhaps sometimes members can be deliberately excluded. Family trees can be pruned to remove any branches that are considered less than respectable. Perhaps this was a person who may have squandered the family money, perhaps had mental health problems, suffered with an addiction, or maybe got pregnant outside of marriage. Where someone was considered to have brought disgrace to the family, they were conveniently forgotten about. This deliberate way of not acknowledging someone is a kind of dis-membering and can result in a failure not to get to know a part of ourselves.

At a time of serious illness, patients often want to reinstate these family members to the family tree. They have had this time to reflect and may have found compassion for these people or have realised that now is the time for forgiveness. It's a time to bring wholeness to their lives.

This 'dis-membering' can also happen to the inner self, as throughout our lives we can focus on moving forward and may end up leaving rejected, disowned parts of ourselves behind. But we need to look towards ourselves and others with great respect and reverence and do what we can to look at the whole of ourselves and our families in order to find true self-awareness and peace.

In more recent times, we have come a long way from the knowledge that what we don't know can't hurt us, and that all that happened before we can remember will not affect us. However, we

Lessons from a Bedside

now know that it is precisely what we don't know that can indeed affect us the most and influence the quality of our lives, including our ability to deal with loss.

Sam's Story

Walking down the corridor, I observed Sam leaning against the door to his bedroom looking as though he was in need of attention.

'Are you okay, Sam?'

'I would like to go to the smoking room for a cigarette, please,' he replied.

Sam had been a patient with us for a few weeks at that time. He had a mop of red hair and his glasses were always perched on his nose, giving him the look of an ancient, wise scholar. Born in London in the sixties, he had lived the life of a wanderer throughout the world, working in the field of engineering. He had grown up in the upper echelons of London society, in what many would regard as a life of untold privilege and comfort. He had settled in Ireland ten years earlier – he preferred the anonymity that Ireland offered him – and he was a quiet gentleman who found being confined with a serious illness both debilitating and restrictive.

Sam was frustrated that he had poor physical energy, and yet his mind was always active, with a deep need to keep moving. As had been the case for most of his life, his spirit was restless.

'As a young child, I was very energetic,' he reflected one afternoon. 'I didn't like early school. I found it boring and unstimulating. I was disruptive and many times my parents were called. I was sent to boarding school at the age of ten, and I felt it was because my parents needed me out of the way.' His voice faltered a little at this point. 'Away from them.'

Clearly, this had a profound effect on how Sam experienced life, although he was to find an element of freedom in his college years.

'I'll be honest, when I discovered drugs, I found a world I could escape to, and almost be myself,' he admitted. He wanted to carve out a life of his own, and his quest to find himself came at great cost, in that he had little contact with his family and friends.

After college, Sam travelled, finding sporadic work when and where it suited. He returned home to London only occasionally. 'I was the black sheep of the family,' he said. 'I didn't measure up to my parents' expectations.'

He described himself as a little eccentric, preferring his own company. Being diagnosed with cancer in his mid-fifties was a real shock for Sam. It took him over six months to let his family know. He had requested no fuss, and that they just let him handle his illness in his own way. There was little family contact, although one former engineering colleague, Kevin, visited him regularly.

Due to ill health, Sam resigned from work and began to visit his local library, revelling in the comfort and peace that reading brought him.

Later, we talked through his need around end-of-life care. He was insistent that his family be informed of his death afterwards.

'And what of a funeral?' I threw out to him.

'I don't think anyone would come to my funeral,' he said, almost to himself. 'And besides, who would organise it?'

'I'll organise a funeral for you, Sam, and I'll attend,' I replied. My tone was light, even though I very much meant it. I didn't want Sam to get a sense that I was doing him a favour out of pity.

He had no particular interest in organised religion, but he did find comfort in reading the Christian bible on his visits to the library; he read the book from cover to cover. He particularly liked Psalm 23:

The Lord is my shepherd, I shall not want.
He makes me lie down in green pastures;
He leads me beside still waters;
He restores my soul
He leads me in quiet paths
for His name's sake. (1-3)

After further discussions, Sam noted that he did wish to have small private funeral service. 'It would be a nice ending,' he whispered. He asked that it be held in the local funeral home, away from a church, and that I would lead the service.

One dark, bitterly cold afternoon, we talked through the specifics of the service. On his bedside locker, there was a hardback book – *The Inferno of Dante.*

'There's a piece here that really speaks to me,' he said, flipping open the book. 'I would like it read at the service please.

'Midway on our life's journey, I found myself,' he read aloud, 'in dark woods, the right road lost. To tell about those woods is hard – so tangled and rough.'

He thumbed through the book to find another passage: 'Savage that thinking of it now ... I feel the old fear stirring; death is hardly more bitter. And yet, to treat the good I found there as well.'

He picked two pieces of music for the service: 'Amazing Grace' and 'You Are Loved', a song by Josh Groban, a singer who was constantly playing in the background in his room.

I did up a little service booklet, and took it to Sam. Holding it in his hands, he said simply: 'I hope people will come.'

Sam died late in the afternoon on Christmas Day. His old colleague Kevin and I began to organise his requests for a simple funeral service. On 27 December at 4 p.m. in O'Flaherty's funeral home, fifteen of Sam's former colleagues, and their families, poured into the room. Around forty people in all came to say goodbye to their Sam, in what was a very uplifting and beautiful service. Sam's sister travelled to Dublin to be present for his cremation and to bring his ashes home for burial. His mother made contact with us at hospice through Kevin and requested a copy of the funeral service booklet. In particular she wanted to know the pieces of music.

My understanding is that because Sam didn't fit in as a child, he found it difficult to fit in throughout his life. His early conditioning coloured that for him, and yet he was a very lovable and interesting man. He had felt rejected by his family, even if that hadn't been their intention, and he hadn't felt able to reconnect with them in the years that followed.

This reminded me that there has to be a world that accepts all. If we don't fit into the perceived norm of a family, there has to be a way for everyone to belong. We often have a narrow focus and perception of what a person 'should' be. We reject what we don't like or value very easily in others, and we don't give enough thought to how or why we do that. But the richness that we can learn from people different from ourselves can give us a broader world view and can teach us a lot more about ourselves. Accepting the 'pruned branches' within our own family tree can afford us a beauty that is far beyond even ourselves.

The following is a true story told to me by the late Father Des O'Malley, Order of Friars Minor:

An Irish priest based in Australia received a phone call late, on very dark and wet night, asking him to visit a family who needed some spiritual assistance, about ten miles away. Having driven for some time he found himself lost on a backward dirt road. Desperately looking for some sign to get him back on track, in the distance he saw smoke billowing from a chimney in a distant house. As he came closer, he noticed it was a rundown shack, with the door ajar.

He went to the door and called out, 'Is there anyone there?' In the distance he heard a faint voice call, 'Please come in and help me.' He pushed the door open and in the distance saw a feeble-looking man stretched out on a straw bed. He went to his side and enquired if he was alright. The old man looked up at him and said, 'Are you a priest?' The priest answered that he was, and that he had lost his way from the main road. He had gone off track for many miles. He noticed that the man had an Irish accent, and asked, 'Are you Irish?' The old man invited him to sit with him. 'I'm Jimmy, I'm Irish,' he said, 'but I have not seen Ireland since I left it about fifty years ago.

'I'm dying, Father,' he said. 'I have been asking God this past few days to send me a priest before I die, to give me the Last Rites.' The priest looked at him in amazement and said, 'You know I just found you by accident. I got lost trying to find a house that seems to be miles from here.'

He prayed with the elderly man and gave him the Last Rites. Then as they chatted about Ireland, the priest asked where he was from in Ireland and if he had family. 'I come from Mayo,' he said. 'I left it a long time ago, I was working on the bridge road that was built to link Achill Island to the mainland. After that, there was no work at home, so a few of us came to Australia. I found it difficult to find work, so I worked whenever I could on farms. I got to like the local brew, the moonshine, and I just ended up living out here in the outback.'

'God has answered your prayer tonight,' the priest said. 'You must be very close to Him.'

'Indeed I'm not,' said Jimmy. 'I have not been inside the door of a church for a very long time. But you know there is one prayer that I do remember from my youth,' he continued.

'When we were building the bridge road from Achill, many, many years ago, we had a very kindly foreman. Every day when the local church rang out the Angelus bell at twelve in the day, this foreman would ask us to down the shovels and say a prayer. I have never forgotten that, and when I hear a church bell, it reminds me to say a prayer.'

Listening attentively, the priest asked, 'What was the name of the foreman?' The man answered, 'His name was John O'Malley.' The priest looked at him with shock and surprise, and said, 'That man was my father.' They spent the night together, talking of Ireland. The elderly man explained, 'I have had no contact with my family since I left Ireland – I wasn't great at the writing.'

He asked, 'Father, will you contact my family, tell them I'm sorry, I have never forgotten about them. I'm sure my parents are dead now. Since I got sick, I think of home and my family a lot. I'd like them to know you met me and that we talked about them. The years have gone fast, I wonder do they ever think about me?'

Jimmy continued, 'Father, will you give me a church funeral? And I have a little cross here in my pocket, would you send it my family in Mayo please? I would like to think I'm still remembered.'

I have always remembered this story as it says so many important things about family. The man grieves the absence of his family from his life but also holds onto traditions he has learned from them, such as the prayer he was taught in his youth. In these last moments, he remembers them and wants them to know that he remembers them, that they have remained important to him even during times when he hasn't been in touch. And he hopes that he has been remembered by them also. As for the priest, he learns in this moment how his own family have had an impact on the world that even he may not be aware of – a simple tradition his father shared with those he worked with is one that this man held on to throughout his life, recognising its value.

Traditions can be so important in families, a way of sharing something with people you may not even have met but who are a part of you nonetheless. And there are many types of families, of course.

When someone is reaching the end of their life, they often focus on the connections they have had with others throughout the years they have spent on Earth, and how they fit into a wider community of people. Often these thoughts about communities are rooted in family, whether it's the family they have come from or one they have created during their lives. And they might also think about what they are leaving behind: traditions for those who come after them.

CHAPTER 11

Supporting Families and Loved Ones

As a result of the vision of Dame Cicely Saunders, who established St Christopher's Hospice in London in 1967, the modern hospice movement created a realistic hope that nobody has to die alone or with untreated pain. The goal of hospice is to give a person the best possible quality of life, offering physical, emotional and spiritual comfort.

A patient comes to the hospice accompanied by family, a term that means different things to everyone these days. Family can mean blood relatives. They can be relationships through an emotional commitment. They can also mean a person or group with whom the patient feels most connected. Family is mostly referred to as 'next of kin'.

Fundamental to good end-of-life care is the support we give at the hospice to the family of the patient we are caring for before, during and after death. It can be regular medical updates while the patient receives hospice care, as well as spiritual support when needed. And families sometimes just need space and time. A listener to give them permission to speak about what is bothering them.

For most families, an admission of their loved one as a patient to the hospice can be a realisation that their loved one is no longer *living* with cancer, but is now *dying* from cancer. Though the family is already aware of the seriousness of the prognosis and has gone through the many ups and downs associated with the illness, this realisation can still come as a bit of a shock.

It can be very painful, uncomfortable and sad for families to see many physical changes in someone they know very well and love. But it is important for family and loved ones to value their relationship and treat the person who is ill as they always have done, with care and concern. This will help them and help the patient. There's no need to play any kind of 'part' here. The dying will often want to anchor themselves with the familiar, or with the love that they have always known. So family members should just be themselves. It is a very sad time, but it can also be a very fulfilling time. Everyone's experience is very different.

As for the patient, he or she may be experiencing many challenging emotions, such as anger, disbelief, sadness, loneliness and fear. And they are learning to work through them with the support of the medical social work team or the pastoral care chaplains who make themselves available to listen to and acknowledge these feelings, allowing the patient a sense of dignity, a space where they feel accepted as they are.

The patient often has to make adjustments to how they live, and this can often be with great uncertainty. However, they may still continue to set small goals. They might even tentatively want to explore what it means for them to be dying and can indeed test ideas on their loved ones. In my experience, patients can sometimes be very sensitive and vulnerable – they always want to know if you're on the same page as them, and they need you to be, desperately. 'How do you think I'm doing? I feel I'm losing ground,' they might ask. Very often, a family member will say, 'You're doing great,' but what they're really looking for is your honesty. I've said it before elsewhere in this book, but they really long to have that honest conversation. They want to know you're emotionally with them, in the place they're at. They don't want to be taken out of that place. Instead, it may be better to say to them, 'What are you thinking yourself?' Given the chance, they will almost always let you know. Sometimes the silence can do a lot of the work here, and give them time to process things.

Being able to just listen is a great gift. Listening requires time and patience. Allow the patient time to share their thoughts and feelings. Sharing demands listening. For all patients this journey is one they have to make as an individual, but being available to them emotionally through listening can help make this journey a little less lonely.

A loved one who is facing death will want you to talk with them as an equal. No need to worry about saying the wrong thing or that both of you may get emotional. Just be there. Your willingness to be there is what matters and will be a great comfort to them.

It may feel natural to share stories and memories, and you might want to encourage your loved one to do the same. These might just be helpful ways for the patient to say goodbye and you will be glad afterwards that you had these conversations.

But often just being present with a dying person is enough. It might not be necessary to fill the time with talking. Your quiet presence can just be a simple and profound gift for the dying person.

Remember to allow yourself some space and time also so that you have some way of relaxing and expressing your own feelings. This is not an easy time.

When the patient enters the final stage of the dying process they may become unresponsive. However, the patient may still be able to hear what people around them are saying. For the family this is a time of keeping vigil with their loved one. This is a very special kind of presence, one that was considered sacred and unconditional in ancient times. The patient is now beginning to withdraw from this life. The atmosphere in the room changes. A quietness and gentleness descends. The presence of staff is now limited to just the necessary. Family are given the time they need to say goodbye. Overall there is a sense that a very personal event is happening in this room, and that it is a time for dignity and respect.

For families this is a time to include ritual, religious or otherwise. Ritual can guide you all fully into that moment. A ritual like the lighting of a candle to illuminate and signal that death is approaching. The presence of a crucifix to symbolise eternal life. The reading of some favourite poetry or prose. The listening to music to soothe the soul. Prayer to prepare for the transition from one life to another. Ritual can provide spiritual sustenance to mark the importance of the moment of death and can provide a deep sense of peace and acceptance.

Dying is as natural a process as birth. Trust your instincts and know there is a team of professionals you can lean on who can provide important insights into your loved one's physical and emotional changes at the end of their life.

Heather's Story

Heather was a happy little eleven-year-old who bounced into the hospice almost daily to visit her dad, who had been a patient with us for several weeks. Accompanied by her mother, older sister and brother, she would leap up onto the bed to hug her dad, Nathan, a man in his early fifties. He had been unwell for about ten years. Heather liked his spacious hospice bedroom that had a door which led to the garden. She would regularly feed the birds and provide them with saucers of fresh water. She skipped around the garden, talking openly with the birds. She enjoyed doing puzzles sprawled out on the floor, sharing each move with her dad.

Heather was a very familiar face on the corridor of the hospice. She had an endearing presence and would greet everyone by their first name.

'Hi Breda! Hi Olive!' she'd call out amiably, a smile from ear to ear, as she bounded about. There wasn't a person's name in the hospice that she didn't know.

On her visits, after spending time with her dad, she would amble down to the hospice children's playroom. She could spend a long time there arranging and rearranging the toys and books, and making the space her own. It was in this playroom she would meet with the hospice medical social worker, who was available to answer her questions around her dad's illness and his reason for being a patient in the hospice. All conversations were child-friendly and expertly led by Heather.

She particularly liked the evenings when her dad was well enough to go to the hospice dining room for his evening tea. She got to order her favourite – chicken goujons and chips. This was rare as her dad was too unwell most of the time to leave his room. However, when the whole family did get to the dining room together, it was clear that they were very close. There was laughter in the air, as Heather would recount her many mishaps with the animals on their family farm. She would talk of enjoying school, and was particularly proud to have been selected for the camogie team. When she grew up, she wanted to be a farmer, just like her dad.

One morning I visited Nathan and he talked through his sense of guilt around a conversation he'd had with Heather the previous day. The Galway camogie team had won the All-Ireland

Final, and Heather had missed their visit to her school with the O'Duffy cup because she had been visiting her dad in the hospice. Nathan felt she was very disappointed but was hiding this disappointment well in front of him. Every moment with him was precious and they wanted to be together as much as possible during this sad time, but he felt guilty at times that his young and energetic daughter might be missing out on her sporting activities, and other small moments that might afford her life some joy and normality.

After this conversation with Nathan, I talked with staff nurse Megan, suggesting that perhaps we might contact the camogie team management to ask them to visit the hospice to meet Heather and her family. It was a long shot, but worth exploring. Peter, a member of our hospice maintenance team, provided a telephone contact for Gerry Hennelly, the chairman of the camogie team, who was very receptive to our request.

A couple of days later, Gerry and some of the girls from the Galway camogie team arrived at the hospice for this surprise visit with a very special girl and her family. There was excitement in the air with both staff, Heather and family awaiting the O'Duffy cup.

Heather had a couple of hours of pure bliss and excitement meeting her heroes and holding the winning cup in her hands. They came with gifts in abundance; there was the signing of jerseys and hurleys, and stories of winning goals and points. Photographs were taken with the team, proof that might show a family that a dream can indeed come true. The dream of a father for his precious little girl, who would remember this day as a gift from her dad.

Heather asked that the family remain overnight with their dad at the hospice. There was a special event to be mulled over and savoured. At the heart of that event was a dad who drew great comfort from seeing his little daughter bright-eyed with excitement. She wanted to be close with her dad as they shared their stories of the day.

Nathan died three days later. Afterwards, I reflected on the importance of support, not just for the patient but for the family, too. The family and patient make up one unit – they have to be included and considered at all times, both medically and otherwise. This can allow the patient to live with greater meaning, and can also provide a much-needed sense of togetherness for the family.

I also learned from Heather, even though she was barely conscious of her own actions at the time, that being yourself is of paramount importance to a dying family member. She brought the outside world in to her father, without even thinking, and that gave so much meaning to his life. More often than not, there's always time to do something meaningful together, right to the very last moment.

Eileen's Story

Having tea one afternoon in the hospice dining room, I was approached by Eileen. She was in her late seventies, and was a tenacious country lady, with a sense of purpose when she walked into any room.

I had met with Eileen a couple of times as she visited her husband, Paul, who was a patient with us. Paul had been admitted for end-of-life care. I had observed the many family photos in his room and was aware they had three adult daughters. Eileen explained that their daughters were married, and living in Ireland. Eileen and Paul had celebrated their fiftieth wedding anniversary two years before, and all of the family visited for this celebration. Paul had been diagnosed with cancer a year later, and had a reasonable quality of life until six months ago. This was the first time in two years that the family was together again.

Eileen was visibly distressed and tearful as we spoke on that particular afternoon.

'I love my children and grandchildren dearly,' she began. 'But this past few weeks our daughters seem to be bickering and not getting on with each other. I'm very upset about this.'

She talked of the sibling rivalry, with her daughters clearly feeling the need to spend time with their dad but believing that some were spending more time with him than others. With some feeling sidelined, this was a source of annoyance among the sisters.

'They keep snapping at one another,' Eileen revealed. 'They're like children, all vying for their father's attention. I don't want them to fall out and not be talking to each other after their father dies.'

Eileen felt this was also upsetting Paul and her only way of dealing with it was to avoid getting involved in the arguments and to try to keep the peace. 'I just want to have tranquillity in that room, and for Paul to be comfortable.'

She wondered if I would have a word with their daughters.

I spoke to Paula, the eldest, shortly afterwards. Paula was in her late forties, living in Ireland. She and her husband ran a thriving business, and they were a well-travelled, professional couple. I invited the sisters to tea in the conservatory the following morning. She made the necessary phone calls and a time was arranged.

All women were pleasant to me, although a little tension between them was palpable. They were stressed and worried and didn't know how to cope with the onslaught of these new emotions brought on by their father's deterioration. Illness has a way of catching you off-guard in an emotional sense, and I figured this was very much the case for Paul's daughters.

'I've been out of the country for a while and so busy building my business,' Paula said. 'I just feel guilty I haven't had more time with him,' said another.

Yet another daughter, Shelly, noted: 'I only live two hours away from the family home. Why didn't I go home more often to see them? I guess life just got in the way.'

With the strong personalities not necessarily used to being together all at once now that they were adults, and finding themselves in a highly emotional place, they were aware of their rivalry and also aware that they were losing their father and did not know how to handle this. It was their first experience of serious illness and death. Each had their own unique relationship with their father and I invited them to share stories of growing up.

Paula found that he had been overprotective of her when she was young, ensuring that when he took her to school, he escorted her right to the door. The youngest, Avril, laughed, 'When it was my turn to go to school, sure he barely stopped the car to let me out.'

'Do you remember when I had my first boyfriend and he stayed up all night to make sure I got home?' laughed Shelly. 'He made sure to give him a good checking over.'

With the tension duly broken, stories of birthdays, communions and holidays poured forth. They allowed time for tears to be shed and tensions to be dissolved. In sharing their stories, Paul's daughters came to understand that their father loved them all equally but in different ways. They were grieving the father they would lose to death shortly, and that pain was being expressed through anger and resentment.

They felt that talking through their anguish opened a door of compassion for one another. They had forgotten their mother was grieving too, and that she needed them to support her amid it all. After talking through their emotions honestly with each other, they were able to put any resentment aside and create a peaceful family environment for both of their parents. They all got to spend quality time with their dad for the six days before his death.

Stress, sadness and anger are part and parcel of the process of letting go of your loved one. Even walking through the door of a hospice can evoke strong emotions. It's very normal for families to be overwhelmed and frightened by the experience. Oftentimes, family members can project their emotions of anger and resentment onto each other. We do this because we feel it's our only way to express those emotions in the moment. There's really no right or wrong way to express such emotions, but bear in mind that taking it out on a family member can hurt others and can add to their own pain. Being aware of each other's needs, and being kind to one another, can help everyone immeasurably. A little kindness can provide more comfort than you'll possibly ever realise.

CHAPTER 12

Making Memories

Time is a precious commodity. Deep down we all know this, but it really hits home when you or someone close to you has been diagnosed with a serious illness. All of a sudden the daily minutiae of life drift into the background and just the important parts of life become our focus.

If you had one year left to live how would you spend it? How does that change if you only had one month or one week left? Very often when people are asked this question, they don't talk about finishing a project at work or purchasing a new car. They talk of spending this time with family and friends that mean a lot to them. The moments we share with loved ones are the precious memories we keep forever.

Memories are special moments that tell our story, taking us back within seconds to times in our life imbued with special meaning. We remember our past because it has brought us to the place where we are now and made us who we are. Memories allow us to recall the good times and can help us through bad times.

A lot of our memories, especially those from childhood, are sparked by family photographs – many of us have treasure troves of photo albums sitting on a shelf, or these days they might be on a computer or phone. In those pictures special reminders of a birthday, a wedding, a family holiday and much more are captured for us to look back at.

It is also important to create memories at the end of life. This might involve thinking about the people and interests that are important to you, and talking about your goals with your loved ones. If you are receiving hospice care, you could also talk with the team about these dreams and goals. The team can help you figure out a plan to make it happen.

Goals and special memories at the end of a life can come from something as simple as a family meal, viewing a film with friends or tackling a puzzle with a loved one. These gatherings can bring great joy and memories that last long into the future. Special moments like these can be planned over weeks and months, with photographs taken, events recorded and stories and songs shared throughout, all of which will be cherished by families and friends for generations.

Some people also choose to write cards or letters to loved ones – another way to share and record memories but also to leave someone with a personal note to cherish.

Perhaps the most important part of a memory is the emotion it brings. A piece of music can evoke a specific moment of the past and can take us back through the years in seconds and we're once again at that festival. The smell of freshly baked bread can bring us back into our family kitchen and childhood days of returning home from school. Memories can transport us in seconds to a time and place we may have thought we had forgotten.

A memory that evokes a special and beautiful moment for myself is the scent of perfume when I walk through a department store. It transports me back to when I was sixteen years of age and got my first perfume as a birthday gift from my older sister Margaret. It came in a delicate, heart-shaped pink bottle, and had a fragrance of fresh rose, which always reminds me of a time when I was on the cusp of adulthood, feeling grown up and alive with energy, with endless possibilities for the future.

Another memory that floats to my mind's surface from time to time is a bittersweet one: a memory of laughter, ice-cream and breezy summer days with a different older sister, Teresa, on the promenade in Salthill. At the time, she had a summer job as a waitress in Seapoint, and she was sharing accommodation in Devon Park that, thrillingly, I could occasionally stay at. In my mind's eye, Salthill is busy with tourists and we always seem to be heading for the fun fair. When memories of Teresa come to me, I can only allow them in slowly, because somewhere tagging right behind them is another memory, one of holding her hand as she took her last breath.

Teresa's Story

When I was twenty-nine years old, I worked in tourism, and was visiting Dublin for the Saint Patrick's Day parade to work with a group of American marching bands who were taking part. Preying on my mind was the uneasy truth that my sister Teresa was in hospital in Galway. She had been feeling unwell since the birth of her second child, Sarah, who was now six months old, and her doctor had advised a hospital admission for some tests. I was anxious to return to the hotel after the parade to phone my mother to find out how Teresa was. 'Teresa had an operation this morning – she had a breast removed,' my mother reported. This floored me. Though I had been worried, I hadn't expected such serious news and I was now very frightened for my sister.

'I really hope she will recover,' my mother said. 'The children are very young.' At the back of our minds, we knew that something was very wrong here. The telephone conversation gave me limited information, but I had a dreadful sense that this meant cancer, and it didn't sound good.

I returned to Galway the following day with my mind in turmoil. It had been fifteen years since Mamie's death and I couldn't accept the idea that a similar tragedy might happen to our family again.

As I drove, my thoughts were haunted with images of Teresa's young children. Baby Sarah had an older sister, Eileen, who was one-and-a-half years old. I could not imagine what was going through my sister's mind.

Teresa was thirty-five and had been married to Paddy Joe for almost three years. They'd known each other for about eight years, but were just settling into married life, and happily so. Teresa had a free spirit; she knew her own mind and lived life very much as she wanted. She knew what she was about. She was six years older than me, and we were opposites, in a sense. However, we complemented each other well. I was the serious one, always organised, while Teresa had a freedom about her: she loved being out and about in the fresh air, and she laughed almost constantly.

Teresa had a passion for country music, and when we were growing up she had her own personal record player and collection of vinyl records. This music was often heard late into the night from her upstairs room in our family home – more often than not, it was the strains of Jim Reeves. Teresa was pale-skinned, and was very proud of her waist-length black hair. She had her own sense of fashion, preferring to dress casually, but all of her sweaters had to be brightly coloured knitwear that she would order to be made from a knitwear store in the city. Her signature style was her drop hoop earrings in various colours and styles. She accompanied me regularly on Sunday mornings when the roads were quiet as I learned to drive.

Her engagement to Paddy Joe had been low key. They planned their wedding for Easter Monday in our local church, with their reception out of town in Headford. Teresa wore a beautiful white lace dress with a matching veil. It was a bright, sunny day. The whole event felt relaxed; there was no fuss, it was just simple and easy going. I remember duck being on the menu, and it was the first time I tasted duck.

Teresa was creative, enjoyed knitting and was the proud owner of a Singer sewing machine. When she and Paddy Joe moved into their home, less than an hour's drive from where our family lived, she'd spent long hours making curtains.

She settled into married life easily, happy in making a home for both of them.

There was great joy when the newlyweds welcomed their first child. Teresa was besotted with little Eileen, dressing her in colourful baby dresses. She took to motherhood instantly; it was like second nature to her, and she and Eileen were inseparable. Sarah arrived almost a year later. Where Eileen was an energetic child, Sarah was quiet and laid back.

After Sarah's birth, Teresa had often talked of feeling tired and unwell.

'I've no energy, and I'm not sleeping at night, but it's probably to be expected with two little ones who are so close together in age,' she reasoned.

One day she mentioned that she had been planting daffodils in the front garden and experienced severe back pain afterwards that would not shift. We had urged her to visit a doctor about it and after weeks of consultation with him, he advised that she be admitted to hospital for tests. The diagnosis was breast cancer.

After returning from Dublin and visiting Teresa in the hospital, it was clear she was very sick. She was trying to process the news from the medical team that she had breast cancer. Needless to say, she was overwhelmed and concerned about her two very young daughters, being cared for away from their home by relatives. It was a lot of emotions for a young mother to cope with, struggling to absorb bad news while needing to be close to her little girls.

Teresa underwent two and a half very challenging years of repeated chemotherapy and radiotherapy. For most of the time she had a poor quality of life amid the cycle of treatments and hospital admissions. When she did have time at home, she was unwell and needed bed rest. My sister Una, who lived in London at the time, took time away from work and went to live with Teresa and her family for some time to help them out.

Sometimes I would accompany Teresa for hospital treatments and appointments. Driving home afterwards, though visibly unwell, she would ask to stop at a local shop to pick up some groceries and a treat for her little girls: a packet of chocolate buttons. 'Is there a magazine there you would like? Pick one up for yourself,' she'd insist. It pierced my heart so much; she was becoming a shadow of her former self and yet the essence of the person was still there. Her kindness to others knew no bounds.

As her condition deteriorated, Teresa was less able to leave her house. She was nauseous from chemo almost daily and too unwell to have the children in her bedroom. It pained her deeply that she could spend such little time with them. She often talked about how much it hurt her to hear their voices in the distance and not be able to care for them in the way she wanted to.

Teresa spent her final two months in hospital receiving palliative care. This was my very first experience of seeing what palliative care was all about, at close range. It eased her physical pain through receiving morphine. Allowed her a quality of life to be able to move about a little and to have chats with family and friends. The medical team was constantly at her bedside, graciously offering medical support when needed, keeping Teresa's family updated about her condition at all times. At times it was very scary, seeing her in so much physical pain and feeling utterly powerless. She was very brave during visits, although it was clear that it was unbearable for her to be separated from her little girls, and she would become very upset at the mention of their names. She'd had such little time with them before her cancer diagnosis. Being so unwell, she didn't get to experience the carefree pleasure of seeing them take their first steps, their first words, baby cuddles and chats. Before she'd been admitted to hospital, bedtime stories and tucking in were occasional rather than the norm.

For her final Christmas, and aware that the end of her life was close, Teresa asked to return to our family home. The image of Teresa coming through the front door is always painful for me to revisit. She was so slight, so terribly thin, visibly in physical pain, and having lost her mobility she was now in a wheelchair. Yet through all of this she managed a smile.

We hoped that Christmas would be ... I'm not sure what. We hadn't talked much of Christmas that year, but we ordered a goose anyway, and we were going to try as best as we could to have some kind of celebration. Because of her physical pain, Teresa had to take a lot of medication and so when not awake with pain, she slept most of the time. Our house was quiet and had none of the festive feeling of Christmas. We were happy to have Teresa with us and we dared not think past the present moment. Christmas Eve Mass was said especially for Teresa in our local church, and the goodwill and kind wishes of the local people reinforced the reality of what lay ahead.

Teresa had a very difficult and painful Christmas Eve night and we waited for the tiniest sliver of dawn light, so that we could contact her doctor. On that frosty Christmas morning the doctor arrived and, after spending time with my sister, apologetically said with a shake in his voice, 'Poor Teresa is not well. I'll have to call an ambulance.'

The ambulance arrived quietly to our front door. It took time to settle Teresa's pain and to gently ease her onto a stretcher. One moment stands out in my mind: as the ambulance crew carried Teresa from the bedroom, I saw my father standing in the distance quietly, looking so tired and almost stooped over. Teresa, being the gracious person she was, attempted to raise her head towards him. 'Bye Daddy,' she called out. They were the last words that I heard from her. My mother, finding it too difficult to see her leave, went around to the back of the house. I cannot imagine the pain of my parents seeing for the second time one of their daughters close to the end of her life. Una and myself followed the ambulance by car and spent Christmas Day with Teresa. There was no goose eaten, and there was no Christmas that year.

Teresa drifted into unconsciousness and became unresponsive over the next few days. Her husband, Paddy Joe, and we, her siblings, kept daily vigil at her bedside. This was a very lonely and painful time for all of us, but in particular for Paddy Joe. Exhausted and weary, he spent endless hours and days at the bedside of his young wife and carried the worry and concerns for their two young children, now four and three years of age.

Teresa passed away on 9 January, at 8 p.m. She was thirty-seven years old. Paddy Joe had gone to our home, which was closest to the hospital, for something to eat. My sister-in-law Monica and I had been with Teresa as she'd taken her final breaths. A kind and sensitive nurse had quietly placed a crucifix and lit a candle at her bedside.

'If you would like to hold Teresa's hand, I think her time is very close now,' she'd said quietly. No one or nothing can prepare you for that moment. Although you are waiting for it in some sense, it is so final, and happens in the blink of an eye.

Then a few minutes later, 'She's gone, I'm so very sorry,' the nurse said. More than anything, I felt an incredible depth of sadness in that moment.

We had no idea what to do next. We phoned

home and aimlessly drifted out into the cold dark night. Teresa had died, and it felt like the world had stopped moving.

The day of her funeral was bitterly cold and it felt so difficult to see Teresa's coffin being lowered into the cold January earth.

Fifteen years later, again on 9 January, Teresa's husband Paddy Joe died on her anniversary. He too had a cancer diagnosis. Eileen and Sarah, now teenagers, and I were at his bedside as he passed away. While the moment was undoubtedly painful, I was a little bit more prepared, and a little more mature. But when Paddy Joe went, I was hit anew by the sense of unfairness.

At Paddy Joe's funeral Mass the priest recalled seeing Paddy Joe come to him every year to book Teresa's anniversary Mass. 'This year, he went one step further and he went to be with her for her anniversary,' the priest observed. The girls drew great comfort from this.

To revisit a painful memory is not at all easy. In my working life, I've been so used to accompanying people through their final weeks, days, hours and minutes. I've helped countless families on this, their toughest journey. But the pain of loss is so unique to each individual, and years of immersing myself in this part of life doesn't make it any easier to grieve for my own loved ones and to revisit memories, some of which are very painful. Every time I'm with a young mother in hospice, I always see a brief flash of my sisters as young mothers. I am so conscious I need to park the memory in order to be available fully to the people in front of me. However, I allow myself a few moments to remember my sisters when time allows, quietly, before leaving the hospice on such days. Or it can be a visit to the nearby beach to sit and remember them fondly.

Much of this book is about dealing with the agonies of loss and of processing grief, the most difficult, complex and painful of emotions that the human heart will ever have to withstand. I've seen that it's the one pain that will break the heart. And here, I have to acknowledge my own humanity and respect my own pain. Though I am available to people emotionally, I am also a human person who feels that pain acutely, too.

And grief will find you, when you're ready to face the pain. For days, I struggled with writing this chapter and recalling my memories of

Teresa. I put it off for as long as I could, then realised there was nothing left to do but to face it head-on. I picked over the memories tentatively at first, until they became so vivid it was almost like being back there again. While there was love and laughter to be found in those memories, there was also that agony of a final letting go. On realising it again, I sobbed for some time. To immerse yourself in those memories is unbearable at times. But it's better to go through them rather than hover around the feeling.

After I finished this final chapter, I sat down with my memories and a cup of tea. It was kind of like I'd found myself again. I'd lost myself in the memories, and what followed was a sense of gratitude that I had finally honoured my sisters as part of this book. After all, they are my family and shaped me in some way into who I am.

Grief has a way of finding you when you are ready to face the pain of losing someone who shared your life and still holds a very special corner of your heart. The lesson is to be alert to those times, though difficult to face. And remember, to tell your story, no matter how painful, is to heal.

CONCLUSION

Strange and difficult times are forced upon each one of us throughout our lives (the coronavirus pandemic an obvious and unusual example of this), and as the sands shift beneath our feet, it can be frightening and lonely to realise how vulnerable and fragile our lives are, how uncertain the roadmap for our future might be.

I believe these challenging times, where we're often removed or distracted from our busy and active lives, thrust us into a time of deep personal reflection, where we face the truth of ourselves and the world around us in a new and different way.

In our world that rewards the individual who soars to the greatest heights, it takes real courage to stare down your own limitations and find happiness in your achievements, no matter how humble. When the odds are stacked against us, we find out who we truly are. I believe there is a spark within all of us that will ignite when the pressure is on. We experience this daily in the stoic courage of ordinary people dealing with big challenges in life who somehow find the strength to hang in there when they have every reason to give up. It can be somewhat easier to drift into the mindset of doubt than to take those decisive steps towards making new goals happen. The answer is simple: find out what you truly love to do, then direct your energies into those pursuits that make all this possible. While scary, uncertainty can also provide space and time to re-evaluate our lives and indeed our values.

Perhaps in these breakneck modern times, we too will allow time for our souls to catch up with our lives of daily living. Maybe ask ourselves the question – How would you live differently if you had a second chance? You should not just change things on the outside, but also within. In a time of collective vulnerability let us practise compassion for self and others.

Amid the coronavirus pandemic, emerging through such uncertainty, was a deep sense of kindness, compassion and empathy towards each other, in our families, our places of work and our communities. Despite all the darkness of this time, human hope was based on the instinct that at the deepest level of reality some intimate kindness holds sway. In all of our confusion, fear and uncertainty, we called upon kindness to come and support us and open pathways of possibility by activating in us our invisible potential. These days, we have little idea of the effect we actually have on each other. Though we know each other's faces, we never know what destiny shapes each life. Because we are so engaged with the world, we can easily forget how fragile life can be and how vulnerable we always are.

A hospice environment is a constant reminder of the fragility of life. Stop and think for one moment that somewhere someone's life has just changed, irrevocably, permanently and not for the better. Everything that was once so steady, so reliable, must now find a new way of unfolding.

Such is the story of many through these uncertain times. However, the kindness of others can in great measure bring healing and hope to many. I have witnessed this many, many times through my hospice work.

Our healthcare assistant Regina, who often has come to work early in the mornings to style or colour patients' hair for a particular occasion, brings vivacious delight and good humour to so many on a daily basis. Simon, who accompanies many male patients for their daily shower, will sensitively ask if they would like some aftershave cologne. Then there's Gerry, who delights in offering the patients a jacuzzi, together with candlelight and soft music. Trish brings calm and peace through her soft singing as she goes about her daily work as a healthcare assistant – in particular, her rendition of 'Galway Bay'. My fellow chaplain Dave has a real gift for corridor conversations with patients and families, meeting them exactly where they are at in their daily challenges. Occasionally, he will offer a patient a stroll in the garden or a visit to the sea. Megan and Olive, both nurses, have the capacity to sense what is not being verbalised by our patients, and will enquire of Dave and me, if perhaps we can arrange a movie night or a pizza evening for a family to create a special memory with their loved one. There is Doctor Orla, who is always so selfless with her time when it comes to giving an empathetic ear to patients and their families. I think of our good-humoured healthcare assistant Patricia, who is so gracious and sensitive to the needs of all patients. There's Dina, who always ensures that every room is spick and span and freshly scented for the arrival of new patients. And then there's staff nurse Norma, who has a special gift of knowing when anniversaries and birthdays need to be celebrated for our patients. And finally, we are lucky to have John Meehan, a hospice volunteer, who is constantly available to transport our patients and their families for special occasions in his Mercedes, even going so far as to give them a colourful guided tour of their surroundings. He's a man who certainly knows the value of travelling in style. All the people who work here bring their own unique gifts as we support each other to bring our patients on this, their final and most important journey in life.

I've realised that the old Irish proverb still rings true. 'Ar scáth a chéile a mhaireann na daoine.'

'In the shelter of each other, the people survive.'

ACKNOWLEDGEMENTS

Writing *Lessons from a Bedside* was harder than I thought and more rewarding than I could ever have imagined. I'm forever indebted to the many people that helped make this happen. My deep gratitude to Aoife Nally whose encouragement to write this book gave me the belief and energy to make it possible. Trudi Fallon who was always available to offer advice and rescue my spirit in times of technical glitches. My fellow chaplain Dave Cribben whose sound advice and good humour kept all in perspective.

My very lovely friend Regina Luft, who would enquire regularly 'How's the book going?'. Dr Orla Geaney and Dr Leona Reilly who have beautiful capacity to lift the human spirit with their words of encouragement. My good friend and hospice volunteer Mary Lally, who has been available to support pastoral care in the small and big events through the years. Joan Kelly who with jovial good humour ensures there is plenty of 'words to heal the soul' available regularly. Berney Walsh, at all times enquiring, 'Is there anything you want me to do?' My sincere gratitude to all the staff and volunteers at Galway Hospice – you have brought a wholeness to my life.

Palliative medicine consultants Dr Ita Harnett, Dr Camilla Murtagh and Dr Eileen Mannion, whose wise and kind presence brings balm and comfort to the soul.

A very special thank you to Sinead Cassidy and Triona Barrett who sponsored many special events for Galway Hospice at The G Hotel. Your kindness brought such comfort to our patients and families.

Mary Nash, CEO at Galway Hospice, for writing the foreword to this book. Thank you most sincerely for your support and your open door for the many chats.

A sincere and heartfelt thanks to the amazing team at Hachette Ireland. Joanna Smyth, who listened to my initial conversation and heard what was being said beyond words. Ciara Doorley, whose sensitivity and graciousness around the inspiring stories of the hospice patients ensured that all were heard and written with deep respect. Tanya Sweeney, for her keen insight and support in bringing the stories to life. Susan McKeever, for her wise guidance through the text. It is because of your efforts and encouragement that *Lessons from a Bedside* reflects the gracious and holistic care of the hospice.

To my family, who in the shelter of each other we have grown: Mickey, Margaret, Eileen and Una. Sister-in-law Monica, for her kindness and support. My many wonderful nieces and nephews, it is a privilege to be part of your lives. In memory of my sisters Mamie, Teresa, Berney and Ann. I'm lonesome for all the conversations we never had.

Bishop Brendan Kelly, who makes himself available annually to celebrate our hospice Remembrance Mass. Your support and kindness is very much appreciated. Fr Michael Mulkerrins, whose absence from the hospice is felt deeply at this time. Fr Martin Glynn and Fr Jose Thomas for their generosity of spirit in offering the sacraments to the patients at the hospice.

But most of all my deepest gratitude goes to the patients and their families at Galway Hospice, who have afforded me the great privilege of being a chaplain to them. You will always hold a special place in my heart.

Remembering in a special way the patients whose stories have inspired this book, and their families. My heartfelt thanks to Harry and Moya O'Donnell, Anne and Dermot Moran, and Marie, sister of Caroline Egan.

To Nicola Purcell, who listened to her inner voice and made that telephone call in January 2010. You opened the door to Galway Hospice for me, and for this I am eternally grateful to you.